"Unseen Footsteps of Jesus"

OLAM HABA

(Future World)

Mysteries Book 3-"The Sunrise"

JERRY AYERS

authorHOUSE®

AuthorHouse™
1663 Liberty Drive
Bloomington, IN 47403
www.authorhouse.com
Phone: 833-262-8899

© 2023 Jerry Ayers. All rights reserved.

No part of this book may be reproduced, stored in a retrieval system, or transmitted by any means without the written permission of the author.

Published by AuthorHouse 02/01/2023

ISBN: 978-1-7283-7821-3 (sc)
ISBN: 978-1-7283-7819-0 (hc)
ISBN: 978-1-7283-7820-6 (e)

Library of Congress Control Number: 2023901776

Print information available on the last page.

Any people depicted in stock imagery provided by Getty Images are models, and such images are being used for illustrative purposes only.
Certain stock imagery © Getty Images.

This book is printed on acid-free paper.

Because of the dynamic nature of the Internet, any web addresses or links contained in this book may have changed since publication and may no longer be valid. The views expressed in this work are solely those of the author and do not necessarily reflect the views of the publisher, and the publisher hereby disclaims any responsibility for them.

CONTENTS

Chapter 1 1
Chapter 2 14
Chapter 3 27
Chapter 4 39
Chapter 5 52
Chapter 6 65
Chapter 7 77
Chapter 8 89
Chapter 9 101
Chapter 10 116
Chapter 11 126
Chapter 12 141
Chapter 13 151
Chapter 14 168

1

...the sound of a newborn wailing pierced the silence of the night air. At that very moment the piercing light that had brought pain and suffering to the evil minions of the dark lord disappeared. All the power of darkness that could be mustard failed to stop that beacon of light of Yahuah from descending upon the earth. Satan let out an eerie bone-chilling scream from the black pits of the world of darkness which summoned the demonic vulture of death that was looming and hovering over the capital city of Yruwshalaim (Jerusalem). The demonic minions which had lodged in the Palace of Herod and responsible for torturing the mind of the king followed in the wake of the massive black wings of the vulture of death. With great speed they returned to their dark master and the smoking cauldron of the evil one.

The wife of Ger'shom cut the umbilical cord after the rest of the delivery took place and immediately washed the wailing infant with warm water. Then she rubbed the skin of the newborn with a mixture of salt, honey and olive oil to remove the remaining amniotic fluid and placenta leaving the baby's skin tight and very soft to touch. Next the infant was swaddled with strips of cloth made from an extra dress that Miryam (Mary) had packed and was placed between the new mother's breasts. The wailing ceased as the newborn baby suckled its first meal of milk. Tears of elated joy streamed down the sweat covered cheeks of Miryam as she looked into the face of the newborn child of Yahuah. Then she quietly whispered Ysha'Yah (Isaiah) 9:6, **"Because a lad is born to us. A son** *is given to us and the empire is on His shoulder. His Name is called Remarkable, Advisor, the Almighty Yahuah, Perpetual Father and Prince of Peace."*

The wife of Ger'shom quietly shuffled her way to the entrance of the barn cave and was quickly met by anxious Yowceph (Joseph) and her husband Ger'shom pacing back and forth at the entrance. Yowceph quickly froze in his tracks and Ger'shom grabbed the shoulders of his wife. She peered around the body of her husband and said to Yowceph with a big grin on her face, "*Halal Yah* (Celebrate in praise to Yahuah)! A man child has been born to you!" Ger'shom hugged and kissed his wife and then clapped his hands together as he did a little dance. Then he slapped Yowceph (Joseph) between the shoulder blades and said, "Go in and see your son, my boy! Go in!" The wife of Ger'shom handed Yowceph the lantern and said, "Mother and child are resting peacefully so be as quiet as you can." Yowceph (Joseph) said thank you and kissed her on both cheeks.

With great eagerness and anticipation he quickly and quietly entered into the barn cave and knelt down beside Miryam (Mary) on the bed of straw. His face was full of wonderment as his beautiful wife met his eyes with a proud smile. He placed one of his large hands on the baby in her arms and the other he brushed away her jet black hair from her forehead and gave her a very gentle kiss. They became lost in each other's eyes as they cherished this precious moment and time seemed to stand completely still. The bonding love shared with each other at this special moment in time between this new family of three was so strong it seemed to move the heavens above. The new infant and Miryam (Mary) fell asleep so Yowceph (Joseph) gently took the baby from the arms of Miryam (Mary) and held his sleeping child in his arms for a while. Then he very gently placed it in the crib for animal fodder hewn into the side of the rocky walls of the barn cave and placed his prayer shawl over the infant as a blanket. As he watched the baby sleep in the dim light of the dark cave, tears of pride gently rolled down his cheeks and into his beard. Then he quietly and lovingly whispered, "Sleep, my little son, sleep."

Far to the East in the county of Babel (Babylon, modern Iraq) Master Mag Hammurabi had gathered his fellow magi and their apprentices under the evening sky of twinkling stars for an evening of night-watching. He quickly made note that *Yareach* the moon, *Tsayar the Messenger* (Mercury), *Nogah the Bright* (Venus) and *Shemesh* the sun were gathered in the shoulder area of the constellation of *Ariy* (Leo the Lion) *Yhuwdah* (Judah) and formed a flattened semi-circle above *Regaleo* (Regulus) the bright king star just as the previous night. However, *Tsadaq the Righteous* (Jupiter) New King had picked up speed and at this moment in time had joined in unison *Regaleo* (Regulus) the bright king star creating a very bright shining light in the dark heavens.

Mag Nbuwzaradan from Opis said, "It has happened!" Mag Kadashman from Sippar added, "It has come true!" Mag Belsha'tstsar from Nippur muttered, "I have lived to see the day!" and Mag Zabaia from Erech chimed in, "A major historical event right before our very own eyes!" The apprentices Shadrak, Meyshak, Abed Ngow and the oldest apprentice, Gungunam stood silent with their mouths open staring at the night sky and then looked at Marduk the seven year old apprentice of Master Mag Hammurabi. Master Mag Hammurabi raised his hands to quiet the other magi who were excited about the miracle in the twinkling night sky of the heavens.

"Brother Magi," began Mag Hammurabi, "a new king has been crowned in the heavens. This moment in time, the fourteenth day of *Tishri* (September) in the year of 4 B.C. a new king has been born in the country of Yhuwdah (Judah). According to historical records he is predicted to be one of the most influential and powerful kings of all time such as the likes of David and *Shlomoh* (Solomon) his predecessors. Before the first light of day we shall travel to the west to the great city of Yruwshalaim (Jerusalem) to pay our respects to this new king. Furthermore, before we depart to load the camels for the long journey, on behalf of all my brother magi and their apprentices I want to extend my apologies to my young apprentice Marduk for doubting his natural born instinct and wise insight expressing his talents as a true night-watcher! I am very proud of you, Marduk."

Back to the West in the open grassy fields of *Beyth Lechem* (Bethlehem), meaning 'house of bread', the shepherds were watching their flocks because it was the beginning of the breeding season before the winter rains in the valley and snow in the upper hills. Two times a year the head shepherds stayed with the flocks constantly even sleeping in the open fields under the stars. Those two times were the breeding season in the month of *Tishri* (September-October) and lambing season in the month of *Adar* (February-March). As they sat around the campfire in the fields surrounding *Beyth Lechem* (Bethlehem) they kept guard during the night over their flocks. The glowing wood embers snapped and popped as the shepherds warmed their bare hands from the cool fall night air. The head shepherds discussed the mandatory census, the feast *Chag Ha Sukkot,* the Feast of Tabernacles and even the insanity of King Herod. Then one of shepherds commented on the very bright star *Regaleo* (Regulus) casting down its light rays from the constellation of *Ariy* (Leo the Lion). Its light was magnified more than anyone had ever seen before. It was so bright that it even outshined the light of the moon.

Then all of a sudden right before their eyes a messenger angel of Yahuah bringing tidings came upon them and the glory of Yahuah illuminated all around them and they became frightened with a great fear. The light was so bright that it blinded their eyes and the shepherds fell face first to the ground as if they were dead corps. The messenger angel said to them in a deep reverberating voice, "Do not fear, because I announce good news to you, a great delight which will be for all the people because a Deliverer was born to you today, who is Yahuah as the Messiah, into the town of David. This will be the supernatural indication to you: You will find an infant wrapped with strips of cloth, lying outstretched in a crib for fodder." The shepherds looked up and at once, there appeared with the messenger angel a large number of the celestial angels that could not be counted, praising Yahuah relating in words, "Glory in the highest to Yahuah and peace on the whole globe and delight and kindness among human beings." Even though the words were spoken the very sound of their syllables by this angelic multitude were like musical notes accompanied by harps and flutes, so beautiful, peaceful and soothing.

It came into being as the messenger angels from heaven, the eternal abode of Yahuah, departed from them, the shepherds said to one another, "Let us travel, in fact, to Beyth Lechem (Bethlehem) and let us see this utterance that has come into being which Yahuah has made known to us." The minds of the shepherds were filled by the mystery of this joyous good news so they woke up their minor shepherds and instructed them to keep guard over the flocks while they went into the town of Beyth Lechem (Bethlehem) to search for the miracle spoken of by the messenger angel. The minor shepherds looked at the head shepherds with puzzlement as if they had drank too much sweet wine, however the night was still very early. The head shepherds left their flocks with a quick skip in their steps and excitement oozing from the speech of their tongues.

Since the head shepherds were local they knew that all the inns were full because of the census and it was now the beginning of the seven day *Chag Ha Sukkot*, Feast of Tabernacles. All the major and respectable inns had been booked for months and the streets were packed even at this hour of the night. Yet they were not to be discouraged. The image of the messenger angel shining in the translucent light of Yahuah's glory was imprinted upon their minds and the sound of the myriad of angelic voices praising the Highest of highest rang fresh in their ears. Nothing was going to discourage or stop them from their mission of finding that newborn baby lying in a crib for animal fodder just as the messenger angel had commanded and instructed them to do.

As the shepherds traveled down the narrow dusty streets of *Beyth Lechem* (Bethlehem) dodging and weaving through the maze of animals and fellow humans alike, they would occasionally be stopped by inquisitive passerby's asking why a group of shepherds were roaming the streets instead of being in the fields with their flocks of sheep. The shepherds would respond with the story of the miracle that they saw and heard under the night sky of the fields while they were watching over their flocks. This quickly brought laughter and ridicule from those requesting an explanation of their appearance in town this time of night. The shepherds were not to be dissuaded or discouraged and would quickly resume their search for the miracle child.

Finally, after three hours of diligent searching they came upon a small inn on the outskirts of the town and one of the shepherds energetically knocked on the door. The dull sound of knuckles beating upon wood quickly reached the ears of the innkeeper. The innkeeper snorted, "What do you want? We are full. No room I tell you, no room." However, the shepherds were relentless in their knocking so the innkeeper unwillingly went to answer the door. He cracked open the door a bit as it groaned on its rusty hinges. The dim light from the lantern shown through the crack and the innkeeper could see a group of men in the dim lit shadows of the night with shepherd crooks. The innkeeper quickly said, "Go away! We are full and don't have any room in the inn." Then he began to close the door shut when a shepherds crook was lodged in the remaining crack in the door.

A deep baritone voice said, "Excuse me kind sir. I am *Tsadaq ben David* (Righteous son of Beloved) the chief shepherd of the temple flocks. I along with the other head shepherds with me, are looking for someone and wondered if you could help us?" "Looking for someone you say," replied the innkeeper. Tsadaq ben David continued, "Yes, we are looking for a newborn child laying in a crib for animal fodder. Have you seen a woman in the condition of full time from carrying a child in her womb today?" The innkeeper quipped, "This is a respectable lodging inn and not a charity home for midwives. Besides, what are your intentions once you have found such a strange sight? Is the mother of the child wanted for some crime?" Then Tsadaq ben David replied, "Do we look like a Roman legion to uphold some kind of law?" With great passion he shared the whole story of the messenger angel and the incident in the open field while they were warming themselves from the chill in the night by the campfire.

When Tsadaq ben David, the chief temple flock shepherd, had finished telling of the miracle and the joyous message, the innkeeper was speechless and a little weak in the legs. Tsadaq ben David then said, "So you see we have come to pay our respects and honor this newborn child of Yisra'Yah (Israel)." The innkeeper stuttered, "Uh... uh...this is unbelievable, absolutely unbelievable. Here in this city….. Could it be? No surely not… but what if it is the one?" Tsadaq ben David interrupted the murmuring of the innkeeper, "Sir I don't understand what you are saying. Have you seen such a woman? *Ken* (Yes) or *lo* (no)! We must find this child before the night is over." Then the innkeeper looked at Tsadaq ben David and answered, "My apologies Tsadaq ben David the news is just a bit overwhelming. My name is Ger'shom and I apologize for the unfriendly welcome that I gave to you and your fellow head shepherds. It is just that the constant beating on my door of travelers looking for a place to stay has me on edge from very little rest. There are so many sojourners and too few beds. We did have a young couple come early in the night and are staying in the barn that you might want to talk to. I will show you the way. Please allow me to get my cloak and I will be right back to guide you to the barn."

Ger'shom the innkeeper took Tsadaq ben David the chief temple shepherd and his group of head shepherds to the barn cave. When they reached the entrance of the barn cave he put his index finger to his lips and motioned for the shepherds to be quiet. Then Ger'shom requested, "Please wait here quietly and I will inquire of the young couple if they would mind having late night visitors." With that said Ger'shom stepped inside the entrance into the barn cave with the lantern leaving the group of head shepherds standing in the darkness of the night. However, it was not pitch black because the unison of *Tsadaq the Righteous* (Jupiter) New King star and *Regaleo* (Regulus) the bright king star were casting a light brighter than *Yareach* the moon. The group of head shepherds bathed in this night light resting upon the shepherd's crooks in their hands wondering what information that this young couple might have about a newborn child resting in a crib for animal fodder. They whispered among themselves what all this might mean with a Deliverer being born from a common family like their ancestor David, a shepherd himself, instead of being born in a palace of royal lineage and privileges. Yet, the longer

Ger'shom took they began to wonder if the young couple would share information of the location of the newborn infant. One of the head shepherds even suggested that they move on and continue the search without the information from the young couple. However, Tsadaq ben David the chief head shepherd quickly rebutted that idea and stated that the group was going to wait for the reply of the couple from Ger'shom.

Shortly after that a dim light from the lantern began to cast its rays upon the mouth of the barn cave. The shepherds watched in breathless anticipation as the light from the lantern grew brighter the closer it got to the entrance where they were standing. Finally, the outline of the figure of the innkeeper could be seen through the dim light and they could hear the footsteps of Ger'shom approaching from within the barn cave. Ger'shom stopped at the entrance and said, "The young couple was resting peacefully and soundly from their long and weary travels and I had to disturb their sleep. They make such a beautiful loving couple and they remind me of me and my wife in our early years. Anyway, after they had gained their wits about them I shared your story of what happened in the open fields while you were guarding your sheep. Both of them were so overcome with emotion that they adamantly instructed me to allow you to come in and visit with them because they have reliable information on the great miracle that you seek. They were positive that your search was not in vain."

Tsadaq ben David extended his hand towards Ger'shom and said, "Thank you kind sir and for your troubles and hospitality please accept this Roman denarius (worth sixteen cents and considered a day's wages for a common man)." Ger'shom the innkeeper accepted the "penny" coin and replied, "It was my pleasure. The young couple asked me to convey their one request to you. They have asked that you be very quiet in approaching them as many animals are resting and they do not want a ruckus of clucking chickens, baying donkeys, quacking ducks, baaing lambs and a mooing cow. Well, you get the idea. They want the night to remain quiet and calm. By the way you take my lantern so as not to trip over a sleeping critter because I can find my way back to the inn in the dark." Ger'shom handed the lantern to Tsadaq ben David and departed.

Tsadaq ben David held the lantern up in front of him and the group of head shepherds who entered the barn cave anxious for the information that would lead them to the miracle child laying in a crib for animal fodder that the messenger angel spoke of. As each step bought them closer to the young couple their hearts beat heavy in their chest cavities and their lungs began to breath shallow and quicker in anticipation of finding out information on where the Deliverer was located. Tsadaq ben David very slowly waved the lantern from side to side so that the group could see both sides of the barn cave and not disturb any of the animals. The chickens and ducks were not bothered by their late night guests and kept their heads tucked on their backs and their beaks under their feathers. The donkeys slightly raised their heads when the group approached with their light but then laid their heads back down as the group passed by. Only the half a dozen head of sheep in a small pen stood up from having their four legs tucked under them in the straw and peered at the group of shepherds that disturbed their sleep. A single light shone in front of the group at a short distance with the silhouette of the young couple in the background. It appeared that the husband was standing up to greet the information seeking group while the wife was sitting up on the bed of straw under her. The cave smelled like a barn being musty mixed with the pungent odor of animal feces and body odor that had long permeated into the solid rock walls of the barn cave.

Yowceph (Joseph) was the first to speak as the group approached near, "Shalom, brothers of the Most High. I am Yowceph ben Ya'aqob (Jacob) from the northern village of Nazareth and this is my wife Miryam. We greet you in the peace of Yahuah, the Most High." The chief shepherd replied, "Shalom to you and your wife. I am Tsadaq ben David from this town of Beyth Lechem (Bethlehem). I am the chief shepherd of the flocks belonging to the great temple in the capital city of Yruwshalaim (Jerusalem). First, we must apologize for disturbing your sleep this evening. We come to you tonight in this late hour seeking information about the miracle child that was spoken to us by the messenger angel from the Most High. We will be very grateful and beholding to you for information that would help us locate this Deliverer that was born this evening. Please share with us what you know and then we will be on our way and leave you and your wife alone to rest from your long journey."

Yowceph (Joseph) nodded his head and said, "My wife and I have seen a woman like you described to the innkeeper. She tried to get a room at this very inn but was turned away because it had no room. She was very heavy with child. At the same time I also was looking for a place to stay for my family but was turned away only accepting these humble surroundings for a nights rest from a long and weary journey of travels. It is not the ordinary custom to get involved in the affairs of others so I must ask you to explain why we should believe your story that the innkeeper shared with us and then give you information to locate this woman that was heavy with child? After all we do not want to bear a burden if harm would come to her and her infant child."

Tsadaq ben David raised both arms and replied, "Yowceph we understand you not wanting to get involved in others affairs. However, this matter is not of our own doing but was brought to us by the Almighty Yahuah. Just as the angel told us, I will say to you. Do not be *yagowr* (fearful). We neither mean any harm but are doing just as commanded by Yahuah through the messenger angel. The voice of our ancestor David cries from his grave from the Book of Thillahyim (Psalms) 3:8, ***"To Yahuah is y@shuw'ah*** (deliverance). ***On your people is your blessing."*** Also, 18:50-51, ***"Therefore I will extend my hand in worship to You among the nations oh Yahuah. I will celebrate in song accompanied by voice and the striking of the fingers against the strings of instrumental music to Your Name, magnifying Yahusha the King doing compassion to His anointed, to David and to his seed to the vanishing point of eternity."*** In addition the great prophet Ysha'Yah (Isaiah) said in 25:9, ***"One will say in that day of sunset to sunset, Lo! This is our Yahuah. We have expected Him and He will make us safe and free*** (*y@shuw'ah*), ***This is Yahuah. We have expected Him and we will spin around with emotion and rejoice in His Yahusha."*** The prophet Miykayhuw (Micah, meaning, Who is like Yahuah?) said in his book 5:2, ***"But as for you Beyth Lechem*** (Bethlehem) ***also named Ephraath, too little to be among the clans of Yhuwdah*** (Judah) ***From you One will go forth for Me to be ruler in Yisra'Yah*** (Israel). ***His goings forth are from long ago, from the days of eternity."*** The messenger angel said to us, "*A Deliverer was born to you today, who is Yahuah as the Messiah, into the town of David. This will be the supernatural indication to you: You will find an infant wrapped with strips of cloth, lying outstretched in a crib for fodder.*"

Then Yowceph (Joseph) took a couple of steps sideways and held his lantern towards the shadows of the crib for animal fodder. The figure of a newborn infant could clearly be seen and Yowceph announced, "Here is the miracle child that you seek." Then all of a sudden a bright beacon of light descending down from the union of *Tsadaq the Righteous* (Jupiter) New King star and *Regaleo* (Regulus) the bright king star and pierced the darkness of the cave with translucent light and illuminated the crib in the rock wall that held the newborn infant. The group of shepherds instantly fell down to their knees and placed their faces towards the ground praising Yahuah with loud praises and giving honorable adoration to the newborn infant in the crib for animal fodder just as the messenger angel had foretold in the open fields while they were watching over their flock at night.

2

When the head shepherds had finished giving honorable adoration to the newborn infant called in the Helene (Greek) language *Christos* (Christ) or in the Hebrew tongue *Mashiyach* (Messiah) both meaning "Anointed One" they spread the word concerning what had been told them about this child. All who heard this news were amazed at what the shepherds said to them. Then the shepherds returned to their flocks of sheep in the fields outside the little town of Beyth Lechem (Bethlehem) before daybreak. Instead of being fatigued from lack of sleep, the shepherds were full of energetic excitement as they recounted the entire previous night's events to the minor shepherds who were filled with amazement.

Early the next morning after the sun had risen over the eastern horizon, the baby infant announced to the world that He was hungry and wanted warm milk in His little tummy. Both Miryam (Mary) and Yowceph (Joseph) were awakened instantly and Yowceph got up from the bed of yellow wheat straw. He went to the hewn out place in the cave's wall used as a crib for animal fodder and gently picked up his squalling son and placed him in the outstretched arms of Miryam. As soon as the baby infant found the warm breast of His mother He became silent as He suckled His breakfast.

Shortly after the infant had been fed and was quickly back to sleep, the voice of Ger'shom the innkeeper and his wife could be heard at the entrance of the barn cave. Yowceph returned the infant baby to the crib for animal fodder and joined the side of Miryam as they prepared for the visit of their hosts. Ger'shom was the first to appear and apologetically said, "I am sorry to disturb you because I know it was a very short night leaving you with little sleep and rest. However, I need to feed the barn animals and do the morning chores." Yowceph stepped forward as if to help Ger'shom but the innkeeper quickly held up his arms and stated, "*Lo, lo* (No, no) you don't. Not after the night you just had. You just never mind me because my wife has brought you two breakfast. Now you just enjoy your meal and when you have finished bring the basket back to the inn because I need to talk to you." Then Ger'shom began to attend to the morning chores of the barn animals in the cave.

The innkeeper's wife carried a large woven basket on her head and clung to a red clay pitcher in her left hand. Yowceph helped her with the large woven basket that was covered with a folded cloth. She said to Yowceph, "Now you just sit that down here on the ground and sit next to that beautiful wife of yours as I prepare the table for you." Yowceph obeyed her command and she unfolded the cloth and spread it out next to where Miryam (Mary) and Yowceph (Joseph) were reclining. Then she began to unpack the large woven basket containing the morning morsels. The enticing aroma that flowed from that large woven basket teased their ravished appetites creating a growling sound in both of their stomachs. Miryam let out a little giggle as Yowceph smiled at her while rubbing his own stomach in a circular motion.

First out of the basket was a small wooden bowl full of *labaneh*. This dish was a smooth yogurt cheese spread used for bread crackers or slices of bread. Then placed next to the *labaneh* was a small round loaf of freshly baked *lechem* (bread) with a golden brown crust. Next a wooden platter was removed from the woven basket piled high with *rugelach*. These were small pastries made from rich cream cheese dough and contained a generous mixed filling of various jams, honey and nuts. The innkeeper's wife continued to empty the large woven basket by removing a smaller woven basket filled with fresh fruit of yellow bananas, oranges, red apples and clumps of purple sweet concord grapes. The last item removed from the woven basket a medium wooden platter heaped with a generous helping of piping hot *leshakshek*. This savory morsel was a 'shaken' mixture of cooked eggs and tomatoes seasoned with various spices that tantalized the taste buds. The red clay pitcher was filled with fresh white goat's milk to wash down the buffet. Yowceph and Miryam just reclined there staring in astonishment at the spread out table of food before their eyes. Finally, the innkeepers wife scolded, "Now I don't mind cooking the food for your meal but I am not going to chew it for you! Hurry up and eat before the *leshakshek* gets cold!" With that said, she turned to exit the barn cave and the new parents began to consume the delectable banquet that had been prepared and set before them.

After the large breakfast, Yowceph gathered the empty platters and placed them back in the large woven basket. He gave Miryam a gentle kiss and said, "Now you lie back down and get some rest to gain your strength and I will go up to the inn and see what Ger'shom wanted to talk to me about. I am sure it is about the fee for the use of his barn cave for lodging last night. It was such a busy night that I forgot to pay him in all the excitement. I will settle up with him and then I will try to find better lodging for us until you are strong enough to travel." As Miryam (Mary) laid back down to rest, Yowceph (Joseph) lifted up the large woven basket and headed out of the barn cave destined for the inn to talk to the innkeeper as requested.

When Yowceph reached the inn, the innkeeper was just finishing chopping wood. He motioned for Yowceph to join him and to sit the large woven basket down by the wood pile. Then Ger'shom the innkeeper said, "My wife and I discussed last night a situation that has occurred so I decided to visit with you in private since your wife has been through so much stress in delivering the baby. I did not want to upset her." Yowceph (Joseph) broke into the conversation, "Oh, I know and I sincerely apologize for the error on my part. I hope that you do not think that this incident is indicative of my behavior or morals. I truly am an honest man. It's just with all the excitement and confusion last night I did not think about the sum I owed you for your generous accommodations and hospitality. Just let me know what I owe you and I will pay you now. Please accept my sincere apologies."

Ger'shom began waving his arms back and forth and replied, "That's not it at all. Yes, I do want to discuss my enumeration for the services that you have received but it is not what you think." Yowceph got a very puzzled look and said, "What are you saying?" Ger'shom continued, "My wife and I feel that Miryam should not take the long travel back to Nazareth for at least two to three months so that she can gain all her strength back and the infant child will have time to grow and not be under the stress of traveling at such a young age. Therefore, what we are proposing is that you and your family to join us in the main house and share our room for six more days until the festival of *Chag Ha Sukkot*, Feast of Tabernacles is over. Then we will provide you with a room of your own until it is time to travel home. We do not intend on charging you a single *lepton* "mite" (worth about 1/8 cent). I know you could not see in the dark last night but my wife and I are not spring chickens anymore. The festival has really taken its toll on us this year with the census and all. I can use your help outside and my wife could use the help of Miryam as soon as she is able to put the inn back into order after this celebration is over. Your keep and shelter are a worthy trade for all the work that needs to be done."

Yowceph was stunned at the offer and then explained, "My kind sir, that is a very nice offer and I don't want to seem unappreciative but Miryam has relatives expecting her yesterday in the Upper City of Yruwshalaim (Jerusalem). They have to be worried sick about now since we did not show up last night." Ger'shom replied, "*Ken, ken* (Yes, yes) just worried sick! We must send a messenger right away to the gates of the Upper City and inform them of the news of your where-a-bouts and the new child." Yowceph thought for a moment then remarked, "Miryam is not yet strong enough to travel and the infant needs to rest. I know her grandfather and he will send an entourage for us and remove us immediately to the great city of Yruwshalaim (Jerusalem) and will dote over his granddaughter causing her more stress and unrest. Let's send a message that we are safe but have been slightly delayed and have a surprise to share with him after I am through conducting business. Thus we will meet him at the gates of the Upper City for the feast *HaAcharitth Gadowl Yowm* (The Last Great Day) the day after *Chag Ha Sukkot*, Feast of Tabernacles is over. Therefore, we accept your offer but staying after the festivals to help you I must talk it over with her grandfather to make arrangements to take care of our belongings back in Nazareth until we return back home." Ger'shom nodded his head in agreement saying, "That is a fine plan young man. You are a man of honor. I will find a messenger and send him to you this very morning. My wife will make the necessary arrangements and help your wife and infant move up to the main house before the high sun (noon). Don't you worry none lad. Everything will work out to the divine will of Yahuah. You will see."

Yowceph returned to the barn cave and found Miryam wide awake laying on the yellow bed of wheat straw. He explained the whole offer of Ger'shom and his wife and also the idea of the messenger. Yowceph picked up the sleeping infant in his arms and Miryam said, "Husband you are so wise. We must do something for the innkeeper and his wife in appreciation for their generosity. They have given of themselves to help us strangers even though they have a full inn of guests demanding their attention. Can't we give or do something for them?" Yowceph shook his head and replied, "Ger'shom is firmly set in his ways and has totally refused any money for their provisions to us. I just don't know what we can do." Miryam (Mary) suggested, "Well, we just need to tell grandfather that we are going to stay on for a couple of months because you have a job of carpentry that needs to be completed before we can go back home. That way maybe you can make something for the inn as a way of saying thank-you." "Great idea Miryam," Yowceph said in agreement, "I will speak once again to Ger'shom later this morning and get an idea of what I can make for them." Then Yowceph (Joseph) put the sleeping infant in the arms of Miryam and briskly walked out of the barn cave. After visiting with Ger'shom the second time, Yowceph discovered that the innkeeper's wife had always wanted a large spice bin for the inn kitchen. Ger'shom agreed to let Yowceph make the spice bin as a surprise as compensation for meals and lodging.

As the messenger, who was sent by Yowceph, stood patiently waiting outside the large wooden gates of the Upper City of Yruwshalaim (Jerusalem) he marveled at the large steady flow of the crowded street coming in and out of the gates either going or returning from worship at the temple for *Chag Ha Sukkot*, Feast of Tabernacles. Finally, Matityahu ben Levi (Matthew son of Levi) and *Qatan Yow* (Little Joe), the grandfather and young uncle of Miryam (Mary) arrived outside the gates of the Upper City and then one of the guards pointed out the anxious messenger. Matityahu ben Levi and *Qatan Yow* weaved their way through the river of people and approached the messenger. Matityahu ben Levi said to the messenger, "I am Matityahu ben Levi of Nazareth whom you seek. Let's step to a private and a quieter place away from this mass of confusion." The messenger followed Matityahu ben Levi and *Qatan Yow* away from the Gennath Gate of the Upper City to a less crowded place in front of the white stone wall of the suburb just north of the Upper City.

Matityahu ben Levi then nodded his head towards the messenger and the messenger began, "Sir, I have a message from Yowceph and your granddaughter Miryam from the town of *Beyth Lechem* (Bethlehem). Yowceph has been delayed to conduct important business after the feasts but wanted you to know that they both are safe and sound. He and Miryam will be coming to you in six days to join you for the *Chag HaAcharitth Gadowl Yowm* (Feast of The Last Great Day). They will meet you at the Gennath Gate of the Upper City just before the sitting of the sun in the west. Miryam sends her love and said to stop worrying that she is bringing you a surprise that was hand crafted with you in mind. They also send their apologies to Ya'kov Melek'Beyth Aer (James Henry Ayers) the fan maker, their festival host, and ask for his understanding because the business offer was just too good to refuse at this moment." Matityahu ben Levi stroked his beard with curiosity and then looked at the messenger and said, "Here you go young lad, a Roman *assarius* coin (one cent) for your troubles. *Shalom.*" The messenger took the coin and departed becoming lost in the flowing sea of people on the street.

Very early that exact morning, just before the sun began to peak over the eastern horizon, a large caravan left the city gates of the town of Babel (Babylon modern Al Hillah) in the country of Babel (Babylon modern Iraq). The caravan of Magi consisted of Master

Mag Hammurabi and his apprentice young Marduk from the city of Babel; Mag Nbuwzaradan and his apprentice Shadrak from the city of Opis; Mag Kadashman and his apprentice Meyshak from the city of Sippar; Mag Belsha'tstsar and his apprentice Abed Ngow from the city of Nippur and Mag Zabaia and his apprentice Gungunam from the city of Erech. These wise men of the magicians and their apprentices were on a mission to search out and see with their own eyes the New King in the western country of Yhuwdah (Judah). The king according to their extensive studies and religious order was to be known as the mightiest King of all kings on the earth. Their journey to the capital city of Yruwshalaim (Jerusalem) would take them over 700 miles of desert sand and mountain peaks lasting for twenty-four grueling days.

After a couple of days of rest at the main house of the inn, Miryam began to assist the innkeeper's wife with tending to the needs of the overflowing guests of the inn. The remaining days of the seven day celebration of *Chag Ha Sukkot*, Feast of Tabernacles seemed to pass quickly and was soon to be over at sundown as the celebration of *Chag HaAcharitth Gadowl Yowm* (Feast of The Last Great Day) was to begin. Thus at mid-afternoon Yowceph (Joseph) loaded Miryam (Mary) and the infant baby on the back of the faithful donkey Bil'am and said to Ger'shom the innkeeper, "Thank you so much for your hospitality and generosity that you showed to me and my family in time of need. For now we must travel to the great city of Yruwshalaim (Jerusalem) to celebrate *Chag HaAcharitth Gadowl Yowm* (Feast of The Last Great Day) with the family of Miryam and also perform the *brit milah* (covenant of circumcision) of my infant son. However, we shall return in thirty-three days after the infant has been consecrated to Yahuah at the Temple. Then I shall fulfill the business obligation that I made with you." Ger'shom the innkeeper winked at Yowceph and a big grin could be seen through his shaggy beard as they waved good-by and he kept secret the surprise of the large wooden spice cabinet that he and Yowceph had planned for his wife.

Yowceph and Miryam were fulfilling the Law of Mosheh (Moses) required in the book of *Vayiqra* (Leviticus) meaning 'Yahuah called' chapter 12:2-4, *"If a woman has conceived a seed and has born a young male, then she shall be ceremonially foul, contaminated, defiled and polluted for seven days from sunset to sunset. This is according to the days from sunset to sunset of the impurity of her sickness of personal menstruation; she will be ceremonially foul, contaminated, defiled and polluted. On the eighth day the flesh of his foreskin will be cut short and circumcised. Then for an additional thirty-three days from sunset to sunset she will remain in the blood of her ceremonial purification. She must not touch any sacred thing or place and she must not come into the consecrated place of the sanctuary until the days from sunset to sunset of her ceremonial purification are fulfilled."*

After an hour and a half of travel Yowceph (Joseph) and Miryam (Mary) found themselves at the Gennath Gate of the Upper City. A large crowd was exiting the large wooden gates going home from the Temple after evening prayers. Yowceph helped his wife down from Bil'am the donkey as she turned around while holding the sleeping infant and watching the large crowd navigate through the crowded street. Shortly following a brief wait, Matityahu ben Levi exited the gates and spotted Yowceph and his granddaughter Miryam. Then he began wildly waving his arms shouting, "Shalom Yowceph Shalom." Yowceph looked in the direction of the greeting and gave a simple wave because he could not fight the upstream flow from the crowd of people. Yowceph stayed put as Miryam kept her back to the exiting crowd protecting the infant baby from being bumped and jostled around. Relieved Matityahu ben Levi greeted Yowceph with a kiss on both cheeks and then Miryam turned around and her grandfather saw the baby in her arms. He exclaimed, "How did…where…when did this happen?" Miryam explained, "Oh, grandfather it is so good to see you too! We will fill you in on all the details later. Please just get us to the house of Ya'kov Melek'Beyth Aer (James Henry Ayers) the fan maker." Then the reunited family entered into the gates of the Upper City and headed to the house of their local host.

The house of Ya'kov Melek'Beyth Aer (James Henry Ayers) the fan maker, was all a buzz over the preparations for the *brit milah* (covenant of circumcision) the next morning. Yowceph decided to give the honor of being the *mohel* (circumciser) to Matityahu ben Levi, the great-grandfather to perform the *muwlah* (circumcision). The women were busy cooking and planning for the private family reception following the *brit milah* (covenant of circumcision) and the celebration of *Chag HaAcharitth Gadowl Yowm* (Feast of The Last Great Day). Yowceph of course would do the *barak ab* (blessing of the father) but a *kohen* (priest) needed to be found to hold the infant during the *brit milah* (covenant of circumcision) and to *barak* (bless) the father. This presented a major and complicated problem to resolve.

If the family asked a member of the Sanhedrin to be part of the ceremony then a member of the ruling party, a Sadducee would hold the child. This was a problem since the Sadducee party was an ancient and sworn enemy of Miryam and her dead mother's family. However, if the family chose a Pharisee *kohen* (priest) this would also raise suspicion among the Sadducee party who were close friends of Butcher King Herod. This was not an option at all because King Herod hated the father of Miryam (Mary). Someone from the priestly line of Tsadaq (Zadok) the ancient priest of King David had to do the ceremony. As the three men were groaning and pulling on their beards in puzzlement, *Qatan Yow* (Little Joe) officially known as Yowceph of Ha-ramathayim or as the Hebrews called it Ramah for short and the Greeks and Romans called it Arimathea spoke up directing a question to Matityahu ben Levi, "*Ab* (father), you have told me that my ancestors were once of the Pharisee party. I know that you instructed me not to talk about it except in private but we are among family. Someday when I am of age, I will take my seat on the Sanhedrin but time and age are not a requirement of Yahuah in the Law of Mosheh (Moses). You have always instructed me that it is the matters of the heart that Yahuah is concerned about. Thus what is preventing me from holding the infant of Yowceph and Miryam for the *brit milah* (covenant of circumcision)?"

Yowceph looked at Matityahu ben Levi and Ya'kov Melek'Beyth Aer (James Henry Ayers) the fan maker. This was followed by a long period of silence, glancing eyes and beard stroking as Matityahu ben Levi was in deep thought. Yowceph broke the deep silence and said, "Matityahu your *ben* (son) is absolutely correct. There is nothing in the Mosaic Law concerning the age requirement of a *kohen* (priest). The only requirement for a Hebrew *Kohen* (Priest) is traditionally believed and required to be *halakha* (follow the collection of religious laws for Hebrews including the 613 *mitzvot* biblical law, the talmudic and rabbinic law as well as customs and traditions) requiring the *kohen* (priest) to be of direct lineal descent from Aharown (Aaron)." Matityahu ben Levi glanced at *Qatan Yow* (Little Joe) and then directly at Yowceph (Joseph) and voiced his final verdict, "The matter is settled then Yowceph if that is your decision as *ab* (father). The matter shall remain private thus protecting the family against ancient enemies. What you desire shall be so! *Qatan Yow* (Little Joe) shall be the official *Kohen*

(Priest) for your *ben's* (son's) *brit milah* (covenant of circumcision) tomorrow morning."

The next morning on the twenty-third day of the month of Tishri (Late September-Early October) it was the eighth day when it was time to circumcise the infant son of Yowceph and Miryam. Eleven year old great-uncle Yowceph of Arimathea held the naked baby as Matityahu ben Levi the great-grandfather took the sharp flint stone and preformed the *muwlah* (circumcision). Then Yowceph of Arimathea said, "*Yahuah barak Yowceph ben Ya'aqob ha ab ha 'uwl.* (Yahuah bless Joseph son of Jacob the father of the infant.)" Then Little Joe, Yowceph of Arimathea handed the crying baby boy over to Yowceph (Joseph) the father who then held the baby above his head towards heaven with both hands and said, "Yahuah bless this little baby boy and may you grant me and his mother wisdom in his upbringing. Yahuah brand it upon our hearts and minds to teach him Your ways and statutes and may he never stray off Your path of righteousness as he abides in Your will. Today I dedicate this child to you and You as His Father called His Name Yahusha meaning "Salvation of Yahuah'. This is the Name the angel had given Him before He had been conceived in the matrix cavity of the womb. I lift up praise to You Yahuah. *Halal Yah* (Celebrate to Yahuah)*!*"

The depths of hell erupted in a deafening crackling scream that shook the demonic kingdom in violent tremors from one end to the other. Gruesome demons scrambled to the black lord Satan's hideous call of war in the spirit realm. Eerie red eyes pierced the pitch black darkness as the pungent rotten egg smell of sulfur filled the air thick with the stench of death. Mass upon mass of various evil minions impatiently waited for the dark lord to give them a command to do his dastardly bidding. This New Sunrise had to be stopped from shining upon the lost hearts of mankind. Salvation had to be turned into hopelessness, misery and despair. The dark lord poured his evil into the smoking black cauldron as his treacherous minions screeched and cackled. The black cauldron belched its thick black smoke as it snaked its way towards the great city of Yruwshalaim (Jerusalem).

3

The large caravan of the Magi had started out on what was planned as a simple eighteen day journey to the west with a destination of the great city Yruwshalaim (Jerusalem). However, the black devilish smoke of the belching black cauldron of Satan was determined to stop the Magi from seeking out the "New King" by causing discouraging delays and troubles. First, there was a four day delay in getting adequate transportation to cross the Euphrates River known in the Babylonian language as *Purottu* meaning "the blue river" or in the Hebrew tongue it was called the *Parshez* meaning "to expand". Once they got across the Euphrates River, which took an entire day, they had to spend another day just getting the large caravan organized again for the long journey. Baggage had to be re-checked and inventoried, food supplies rechecked, camels reloaded and final instructions given to the twenty-five men hired to protect and defend the large caravan against the attack of ruthless and barbaric thieves.

Finally after beginning this journey six days prior, the Master of the Magi, Hammurabi and his group of travelers began to follow their guide towards their destination to the west. Tomorrow they would be in the *Nabataean Kingdom*, (modern northern Saudi Arabia and southern Jordan). They would be following the Incense Route across *Nabatea* until they reached its capital city of Petra. Until then they had to cross over five hundred miles of desert containing sizzling hot winds and shifting sand dunes. Their only relief from this scorching torment would be locating an oasis where they could find shade and water from the strings of oases randomly scattered across this loosely-controlled trading route.

After eight more days of steady travel across the blazing desert and moving sand dunes the large caravan found themselves half way across their desert trek with only minor delays of *haboobs*, which were sandstorms featuring walls of sand and wind but only lasting 2-3 hours at a time. Spirits were high after getting much needed rest at an oasis for the night. Then the large caravan set out on their sixteenth day of the journey to see the "New King". The day began with a cool delightful morning but by mid-day the scorching heat reflecting off the yellow desert sand was once again almost unbearable. Suddenly, the guide raised his hand and halted the caravan in its tracks and pointed to the south. The Magi demanded answers for this mid-day delay and as they peered southward their hearts sunk to the burning sands. What they saw coming towards them from the south was a dreaded unpredictable *Shamal*, a sandstorm that could last for days at a time. The servants quickly set up the tents and the camels instinctively laid down close knit to each other.

The only thing the caravan could do for now was to huddle inside their tents and cover their mouth, nose and ears with their turbans to filter out the small particles of irritating and blowing sand. The camp was set up on top of a large sand dune because the densest concentration of sand bounces close to the ground. Seasoned travelers know not to seek shelter on the leeward side of sand dunes because the high winds can pick up huge amounts of sand very quickly and bury in the sand anything that gets in its path of terror. Total protection is needed as the blowing sand is like a sand blaster and can literally take any exposed bare flesh right off of a human body. The caravan had to wait out the horrific storm because traveling in such conditions would not only cause physical danger but imminent death would occur because visibility would be zero and members of the caravan would get disoriented and lost. The only thing that could be done in this situation is to stay covered, stick together and wait until the storm passed no matter how long it took.

After six days of howling winds, blowing sand particles and no sunshine the sandstorm ceased but another storm was brewing inside the restless Magi. They were all grumpy and short tempered with the servants and their apprentices. The physical agitation of the fine sand in their garments, food, drink and bedding did not dampen their spirits as much as the mental agitation of the constant delays and bickering among the servants. Some of the Magi even suggested returning home causing additional agitation for Master Mag Hammurabi. The demonic darkness from the black smoke of the belching cauldron of Satan was overtaking the caravan.

Then seven year old apprentice Marduk spoke loudly as the camels were being loaded. The long faces of the Magi and his fellow apprentices scowled as he began to speak, "Honorable Magi look all around you and tell me what you see." One of the disgruntled Magi growled, "Marduk have you gone blind? There is nothing but tormenting sand as far as the eyes can see!" "That is correct Mag Nbuwzaradan," quipped Marduk. Then he continued to question, "At this moment in time is the endless sand that you see, is it in the same place as it was yesterday and will it be in the same place tomorrow?" Mag Kadashman retorted, "Marduk we don't' have time for your stupid mindless riddles. You know the sand of the desert is constantly changing its location." Marduk took a deep breath and said, "Does the sand choose where or how it is located next?" Then a furious Mag Belsha'tstsar angrily shouted, "Master Mag Hammurabi control the tongue of your young apprentice before he loses it! He has no right to quiz us like school boys in one of Kadashman's classes. We know that the sand is moved by the wind under the direction and will of the Creator!" Brave little Marduk nodded in the direction of his master and replied, "That also is a correct answer. The sand is moved at will by the Creator and does not know where its final destination will be. We also, are like the sand and are moved by the will of the Creator. However, unlike the sand we know our direction which is westward and we know our final destination that was designed in the heavens and told by the stars that our final destination would be Yruwshalaim. It is not our duty to choose how we get there but to stay in the will of the Creator."

The campsite was completely silent with all eyes staring at little seven year old Marduk, the brave apprentice. Then a light pierced the demonic darkness in the hearts of the Magi and their caravan of travelers and Mag Zabaia began clapping his hands together. Soon he was joined by the other members of the caravan and Master Mag Hammurabi grinned from ear to ear through his thick beard. Then he said, "Well-spoken are the words of wisdom from Marduk. Now let's get mounted on the camels and head towards our known final destination like the sand in the wind!" The caravan broke camp and became alive with cheer and hope as the guide began moving the string of travelers towards the western horizon over the endless yellow sand dunes.

Two days before they reached the *Nabataean* capital city of Petra on their thirtieth day of travel, once again gloom attacked the traveling Magi caravan. This time it was a group of fifteen marauding bandits on Arabian horses wielding long sharp cutlass swords. They were no match for the security that was hired by the Magi to keep the caravan safe but they managed to disrupt travel and scatter the camels carrying the necessary food provisions which were also scattered across the desert sand. This caused another two day delay as the servants and the hired guards collected what provisions and camels that they could find. It was estimated that they lost at least twenty percent of their remaining supplies for the trip which could be replenished at the *Nabataean* capital of Petra in two days. The good news was that eighty percent was salvaged leaving the caravan in good spirits.

Petra was a wealthy trading town located at a convergence of several important trade routes. The two most important was the Incense Route and the Kings Highway known in the Hebrew language as *Derek baMelek* meaning "The Way of the King". In Petra the aromatics of myrrh and frankincense were distributed throughout the entire Mediterranean region. This capital city of the *Nabataeans* lies on the slope known in the Arabic language as *Jebel al-Madhbah* meaning "mountain of the altar" or the Hebrew tongue as *Har Hor* (Mount Hor). This mountain contains the burial place of Aharown (Aaron) the brother of Mosheh (Moses) and the caravan would be passing by the Tomb of Aharown (Aaron) as they entered this capital city from the south.

Two days later the large caravan of the Magi did find themselves in the capital city of Petra, a very busy trading center. The Magi spent two days in the city replenishing their supplies that were lost in the desert sand and also purchasing myrrh and frankincense that they wished to present as gifts to the "New King". These would be added to the already intended gift of precious gold turmeric that a designated camel was carrying and heavily guarded by the hired protectors. After the brief stay in Petra the caravan headed north on the King's Highway to the towns of Madaba and Yriychow (Jericho) and then their final destination of the great city of Yruwshalaim (Jerusalem). The remaining journey would take the caravan five days to complete making the total journey forty-one days covering seven hundred miles of testing, hardships and challenges.

Thirty-three days after the *brit milah* (covenant of circumcision) of Yahusha, the days of washing off for ablution were fulfilled for Miryam (Mary) according to the Law of Mosheh (Moses). Thus also according to the Law of Mosheh (Moses) found in the book *elleh shem* 13:1-2 (Exodus) meaning "these were the names", Yowceph (Joseph) and Miryam presented Yahusha at the temple in Yruwshalaim (Jerusalem) ***"Yahuah spoke this arrangement of words to Mosheh, saying, Make, pronounce, and observe as ceremonially and morally clean every firstborn, thus chief, the firstling who opens the matrix of every womb among the sons of Yisra'Yah (Israel) among red fleshed human beings and among large four legged dumb beasts. It will belong and become a possession to Me."*** They also complied with the Law of Yahuah according to the book of *Vayiqra* (Leviticus) 5:11 and brought forth as a sacrifice a couple of cooing turtle doves tied together or two nestling pigeons.

The young family was met by a human being named Shim'own (Simeon) who lived in the great city of Yruwshalaim (Jerusalem). Shim'own (Simeon) was innocent in character and holy in actions and reverenced Yahuah in all circumstances, eagerly awaiting with patience the relief of affliction of Yisra'Yah (Israel) and the Sacred Breath (Holy Spirit) was upon him. It was to him, having been uttered an oracle by the Sacred Breath (Holy Spirit) not to see death prior that he would see the Messiah of Yahuah. He came by the Sacred Breath (Holy Spirit) into the Temple. The parents brought in the infant child, Yahusha so they could do according to the custom of the Law with respect to Him. He received Him in his arms and blessed Yahuah and said, "Now let die Your slave, Master, according to Your Utterance in peace because my eyes have seen Your Salvation, which You prepared before the face of all the peoples, a Light for disclosure to the foreign pagan nations and a Glory of Your people Yisra "Yah (Israel)."

Yowceph and Miryam were struck with admiration at the things being said about Yahusha. Then Shim'own (Simeon) blessed them with a benediction and said to Miryam, His mother, "Lo! This One will lie outstretched for the crashing downfall and the standing up again from the resurrection of death for many in Yisra'Yah (Israel) and for a supernatural indication that will be disputed and refused. Also, the traveling of your vitality of breath will be on a long and broad cutlass saber, in the manner that the inner thoughts and feelings of many hearts will be disclosed."

After Shim'own (Simeon) had departed they were met by a woman. Her name was Channah (Hanna) an inspired prophetess, a daughter of Pnuw'el (Phanuel) of the tribe of Asher. She was advanced in years of many days having lived with her husband seven years since her maidenhood. Then she became a widow up to eighty-four years, who did not leave the Temple with abstinence from food and petitions ministering to Yahuah night and day. Coming upon them at that very hour, she responded in praise to Yahuah and was talking about Him to all those waiting with patience a ransoming in Yruwshalaim (Jerusalem).

Yowceph (Joseph) and Miryam (Mary) returned to the home of Ya'kov Melek'Beyth Aer (James Henry Ayers) the fan maker thanking their hosts for the hospitality of the past thirty-five days. They also said good-by to Matityahu ben Levi grandfather of Miryam and *Qatan Yow* (Little Joe) the twelve year old uncle of Miryam (Mary). Matityahu ben Levi and *Qatan Yow* would be leaving tomorrow back to their home in Nazareth to check on cook and the sister of Miryam, Shalowmit (Salome). However, Yowceph would honor his commitment to Ger'shom and take Miryam and the infant Yahusha back to Beyth Lechem (Bethlehem) to make a fine spice cabinet as an addition to the busy little inn as a surprise for the innkeeper's wife.

Yowceph loaded Miryam and Yahusha on faithful Bil'am the donkey and exited the Gennath Gate of the Upper City and headed south to the little town known as the 'house of bread' before the sun hid itself in the western horizon.

As Yowceph (Joseph) exited the city with his family, all was not well in the great city of Yruwshalaim (Jerusalem). The winding snake trail of poisonous black smoke from the belching evil cauldron of Satan once again engulfed the Palace of Herod the Great. The massive vulture of death effortlessly hovered over the palace walls of stone patiently waiting to sink its deathly sharp talons into the flesh of unsuspecting human beings. Its ugly head and long sharp beak moved side to side as its red glowing eyes peered into the masses below seeking out its next unfortunate victim. The peace and joy brought about with the celebration of the festivals now evaporated into thin air and was replaced with a heavy feeling of anxiety and uneasiness, especially in the palace. King Herod returned to his paranoid suspicions of everyone setting out to kill him and take over his throne. The ranting and raving flowed from his mouth with cursing in volumes and echoed within the palace walls from his bed chambers. As the sadistic demonic forces tormented his soul and ravaged his body he shook with violent tremors and contorted his helpless body from the wrenching pain that consumed his large body.

The large caravan of the Magi entered the northeastern gates of the great city of Yruwshalaim (Jerusalem). The crowds on the streets stopped and stared in wonderment at such an exquisite display of camels, Magi, luggage and all under the watchful eyes of twenty-five very protective armed guards. Since the sun was about to drift out of sight in the western horizon behind the beautiful background of orange, pink and purple hues the first order of business for the Magi would be to find lodging for their group. However, they did not want to stay in the Bezetha District in the city but rather find something in the suburb behind the second north wall next to the Fortress of Antonia where they could seek Roman protection if necessary. Tomorrow they would send a messenger to the Palace of Herod the Great to request an audience with the half-Edomite king. After finding satisfactory accommodations for their large caravan they all ate a robust evening meal and went to bed.

The next morning after breakfast the Magi requested the services of a messenger from the innkeeper and sent the written message to the Palace of Herod. The messenger delivered the message to the Master of Audiences then waited patiently for a reply. Prince Antipas was the Master of Audiences and took the script of papyrus directly to the bed chamber of his father, King Herod the Great. As he tried to hand the papyrus script to Herod the king snapped, "Boy can't you see I am sick? You would just love to see me in a state of death from exerting myself, wouldn't you? If you think you can get my crown that easily, you are sadly mistaken? You read the message to me yourself!" Prince Antipas just shook his head and said, "Yes my king."

Then he untied the papyrus scroll breaking the wax seal and began to unroll the scroll to read its script. He cleared his throat and began, "*To his Majesty, King Herod the Great, ruler of the Hebrew people. We bring tidings of peace from the East and extend our pleasurable greetings to you, great king. We are the leading Magi from the territory of Babel (Babylon, modern Iraq) and have traveled a great distance to desire and request an audience with the great king of the Hebrew nation. Our honorable intentions are to pay our humble adoration to the successor of your throne born within your royal palace walls......*" Instantly, all the color drained from the face of Prince Antipas as he looked up from the scroll. His eyes were met by his father's which were shooting sharp daggers of death. His voice began to quiver and the normal eloquent speech of the prince disappeared and was replaced by stuttering and meaningless stammering. The only audible utterance that could be deciphered was, "Father, oh great king, this must be a hoax. Let me seek the king's vengeance."

Herod the Great continued to stare down the prince and commanded, "Finish reading the script, you worthless piece of camel dung. Do you think I am blind to your bumbling plots and ignorant schemes against me?" At that moment in time Prince Antipas felt the heavy weight of the sentence of death come crashing down upon his shoulders and quickly muttered, "Oh great king this is not true." Herod became more agitated and screamed, "I commanded you to read the rest of the scroll. Are you in insurrection of my throne and willfully disobedient to my commands!" Prince Antipas cowered like a severely whipped dog and finished reading the script that was gripped tightly in is hand, "....*It is our utmost wish to meet with you at your earliest convenience to present valuable gifts to his majesty and his royal heir of the throne of the Hebrew people. We wait for your reply in this great city and are humbly your servants forever, Master Mag Hammurabi, Mag Nbuwzaradan, Mag Kadashman, Mag Zabbia and Mag Belsha'tstsar.*"

Prince Antipas continued to stare at the papyrus scroll but King Herod was sitting straight up in bed with his energy renewed on the thoughts of vengeance against his enemies. Then the king said, "Well, well, well, the youngest prince of my loins. Don't you think it would be a wise idea to invite these Oriental Magi into the Great Hall to stand in front of the great King Herod to investigate this latest threat to my throne?" Prince Antipas knew not to try to reason with his ruthless and blood-thirsty father so he agreed, "Yes, oh great king. I shall stand by your side and dedicate the power of my sword to kill and rid your throne against any threats!" The king stood up out of bed and pointed his crooked finger at Prince Antipas, his son, and replied, "Don't' let that silver tongue of yours think that it can fool me. As long as I wear the crown of this kingdom, you or anyone else will not remove it from my head and take it away from me as long as I can breathe a breath of air in my lungs. Now, send a message back with the messenger that I shall meet our visiting guests from the East in two days."

Prince Antipas quickly and gladly exited the bed chambers of King Herod and sent the return message with the messenger sealed with the royal seal of the palace. Meanwhile, King Herod began the process of perfuming his body to cover up the stench of his rotting flesh while contemplating his next move in obtaining important information from the Oriental Magi in regards to the threat against his crown. He planned the sly questioning of the Magi so that they or those in attendance would not suspect any ulterior motives. He rubbed his cold-hearted hands together and smiled a sly and cunning smile that could be found on any venomous snake.

The day finally arrived when the Oriental Magi magicians from the East were permitted to enter the Great Hall of the Palace of King Herod the Great. After formal greetings, pleasantries and the giving of some fine gifts to please the king, Master of the Magi, Hammurabi said, "What location is He that has been produced from His mother to be sovereign, holding the foundation of power of the *Yhuwdiy* (Jews)? For this reason we saw the star of Him in the East and came to prostrate ourselves in homage, reverence and adoration to Him." When King Herod the sovereign heard this, he was agitated like boiling water and as soon as word leaked all of Yruwshalaim (Jerusalem) became agitated like boiling water with him. King Herod questioned, "What is his name, this new king?" Mag Hammurabi stated, "We do not know his name, we only have studied the light show in the heavens and have traveled many miles to pay our respects. We assumed you knew since you are of the palace and could present this new king to us." The demonic control took over the king in an instant and began shouting, "Out, out, out from my presence. Guards clear this hall. Guards…" The Magi had never seen anything like this before and were in a state of shock at the sight of this unpredictable and unacceptable outrage.

Within two hours of the dismissal of the Magi, King Herod convened together all the chief priests who were mostly from the Sadducee Sect and the legal scribes of the people who were of the Pharisee Sect and he inquired from them what location the Anointed Messiah was to come from the matrix of His mother's womb. They said to him, "In Beyth Lechem (Bethlehem) in the land of Yhuwdah (Judah). For in this way it has been written and described by the inspired prophet Miykayhuw (Micah) meaning "who is like Yahuah", 5:2, *"And you city of Beyth Lechem (Bethlehem) also named Ephraath least coming to pass to exist among the thousands of the tribal branch of Yhuwdah (Judah), from out of you to Me He will come forth to come to pass to exist one ruling in the nation of Yisra'Yah (Israel) and His family have been from ancient times from the days of sunset to sunset of the vanishing point of eternity."* One of the scribes added, "We believe that the new king born in Beyth Lechem (Bethlehem) will issue forth as Commander with official authority and who will tend to us as a Shepherd of Yahuah's people, Yisra'Yah (Israel)." Then once again King Herod cleared the Great Hall so that he could be left alone to think and plot his vengeance against the threat of this "New King".

4

Three days later King Herod privately called the magicians who were visiting from the Orient and ascertained from them the exact space of time of the light show of the stars over the sky. Then he dispatched them to Beyth Lechem (Bethlehem) saying, "Travel and interrogate exactly about the infant and when you find out the details announce them to me, so that even I may come to prostrate myself in homage, reverence and adoration to Him." As Herod watched the Magi leave the Great Hall he smiled an evil smirking smile while he contemplated the final stage of his sinister plan. He was finally about to rid his throne of the perceived threat to his crown. After they received the command from King Herod the Magi returned to the inn where the caravan was staying and began making preparations to travel south the five miles to Beyth Lechem (Bethlehem) the next day. However, after some discussion the Magi decided to prepare the entire caravan and leave early that evening instead of waiting until the next morning. There would not be as many travelers on the road leading to Beyth Lechem (Bethlehem) and its village streets in the early evening hours which would make it easier for the caravan to maneuver. They would find lodging in Beyth Lechem (Bethlehem) tonight and return to King Herod tomorrow. At last their dreams were about to come true unaware that Herod was using them as pawns to carry out his sinister plot of paranoia madness.

Back in Beyth Lechem (Bethlehem) at a secret location Yowceph (Joseph) was putting the finishing touches on the beautiful spice cabinet that he was making for the wife of Ger'shom the innkeeper. The cabinet had a big bin to store fresh ground wheat flour in with an easy tip out front. Above the tip out flour bin was a dozen smaller slide-out drawers to hold different varieties of fresh spices. The bins inside the cabinet could be hidden by two wooden doors on the front which contained a hand carved picture of the little inn on each door. Ger'shom approached Yowceph and said, "Boy am I glad you are about finished with this surprise project. I think my wife is beginning to get suspicious about our comings and goings all day long." Then Ger'shom walked around to the front of the cabinet where Yowceph was working and became speechless. Yowceph remarked, "Well Ger'shom in a few hours we can take this cabinet to the inn and put it in its new home to surprise your wife. Do you think she will like it?" Ger'shom responded with very moist eyes, "*Ken, ken* (yes, yes) it is beautiful and perfect." Yowceph clapped his hands together and said, "Well then you better go and send our wives off to the marketplace so that we can get this into the inn without being caught with the surprise in our hands!" Ger'shom hurried home to do his part of getting rid of the women so Yowceph could do his.

Miryam (Mary) and the innkeeper's wife left the little inn and headed to the market so that they could be home to watch the inn while the men were at evening prayers at the synagogue. Little Yahusha seemed to be content to be swaddled tight to his mother's breasts and the movement of her walking rocked him fast asleep. They had a long shopping list of fresh fruit, finely ground wheat and barley flour, olive oil, nuts, meat and various spices. The other women at the market smiled at Miryam as they passed by. She was a stranger but they knew the innkeeper's wife and wondered and whispered amongst themselves if they thought the wild story of the head shepherds was true. However, some of the older women would shake their heads and cluck their tongues. Miryam and the innkeeper's wife passed the shopping time with conversations dealing with the matter of the young family's departure in a couple of weeks. The innkeeper's wife said, "It is going to be so sad to see you go child. You have been such a help to me around the inn and Yowceph (Joseph) has been a much needed help to my dear husband. Of course what I will miss the most will be holding that adorable little baby boy of yours and listen to him cooing softly. You all have brought such joy to our hearts that words can't explain." Miryam (Mary) replied, "We shall miss you two very much. You and Ger'shom will always have a special warm place in our hearts for taking us in when we were most in need. Our place in Nazareth will always seem to missing something special because you will not be there with us." The two women gave each other a gentle hug and then completed their shopping. Then they headed back to the inn to unload their market conquest.

Once back at the inn the women opened the wooden door and passed through the guest area to the private quarters. Both women were anxious to set down their heavy woven baskets filled with their shopping conquest to give their arms a much needed rest. As they entered the private quarters, there stood Ger'shom and Yowceph with guilty boyish grins shining through their beards and holding up one of the bed quilts. The innkeeper's wife belted out, "What on earth are you two doing with that bed quilt?" Ger'shom was quick to respond, "Can't you see the improvement we made to this quilt. We just knew you would be pleased." Both women sat down their large wicker baskets and Miryam began to unswaddle Yahusha from her breasts acting totally surprised with the situation. Ger'shom's wife said, "That did not answer my question of what are you doing with my favorite bed quilt that my grandmother had made and passed down to me by my mother. Now out with it! What are you doing?" Ger'shom playfully answered, "We men thought that this would be a good addition to the quilt because it was always missing something." The innkeeper's wife began to walk closer to the men holding the quilt with both of her hands on her hips and snarled, "If you two have ruined this quilt you will experience the wrath of a very unhappy woman. I don't see anything." Yowceph and Ger'shom began waving her closer to them all the while laughing. Then Ger'shom said, "You have to touch the quilt to see what we did not just look at it."

She stomped up to the quilt and began running her hand gently across the quilt, when all of a sudden Ger'shom nodded towards Yowceph and both men let the quilt fall to the floor. The innkeeper's wife gasped and said in a quivering voice, "Oh my stars what have you two done?" She became frozen with her hands over her mouth and began sobbing and shaking her head. Ger'shom put his arms around his wife and said, "A special present for my very special wife." She buried her head into his chest and sobbed uncontrollably. By now Miryam (Mary) had joined the side of Yowceph (Joseph) and put a hand on the innkeeper's wife explaining, "We knew we would be leaving in a couple of weeks so the three of us wanted to give you something special to remember us by as our way of saying thank you for such an abundance of hospitality and love that you and Ger'shom have shared with our little family." Then the innkeeper's wife slowly rubbed her hand over the hand carved doors of the beautiful spice cabinet. Yowceph then opened up the doors and showed her all the features.

As the sun was setting in the western horizon the Magi with their apprentices and large caravan began to make their five mile journey south from the great city of Yruwshalaim (Jerusalem) to the little village of Beyth Lechem (Bethlehem). The night air was cool and crisp and the torches of the guards flickered in the slight breeze and made a light flapping sound as the light pierced the blackness of the night. As the normal custom of the Magi they looked up at the blanket of the night sky and the countless stars twinkled against the black backdrop. However, *Regaleo* (Regulus) the bright king star appeared to grow brighter with each step of the large caravan as it grew nearer to the village gates of Beyth Lechem (Bethlehem). All of a sudden the star in the sky which the Magi saw in the East proceeded ahead leading them until it stood above where the infant was. When they saw the star in the sky they became cheerful with a big and high degree of calm delight. As they came into the residence of the family they found to view the infant with Miryam (Mary), His mother. So they fell down and they prostrated themselves in homage, reverence and adoration to Him. Then they opened up their deposits of wealth and treated Him with sacrificial presents of gold turmeric, frankincense and myrrh. Ger'shom and his wife made ready rooms for the large caravan of the Magi to stay the night. As the Magi were sleeping, Yahuah uttered a divinely intimate oracle to them in a dream telling them not to turn back to Herodes (King Herod). Therefore the next morning they retired by a different road to their own space of territory of Babel (Babylon, modern Iraq). Little Marduk chattered all the way back home about seeing the New King.

The next evening as Yowceph (Joseph) was snoring and Miryam (Mary) was snuggled next to him, a messenger angel of Yahuah shown light by a dream to Yowceph laying forth words, *"Rouse from your sleep! Receive near the infant and his mother and run away to vanish into Mitsrayim (Egypt). You be and stay there until I speak to you again. For this reason, Herodes (Herod) the Great is about to plot and seek the life of the infant to destroy Him fully."* Therefore what was uttered was verified by the prediction of Yahuah through the inspired prophet Howshea

(Hosea) over seven hundred years earlier in his book chapter 11:1, ***"From out of the country of Mitsrayim (Egypt) I have called My Son."*** So Yowceph rose up from his sleep and received near the infant and His mother at night and traveled to retire into the neighboring country of Mitsrayim (Egypt).

The black snaking cloud from the depths of hell gathered into a large mass above the great city Yruwshalaim (Jerusalem) hiding the hovering Vulture of Death. The putrid drool from its beak fell upon the palace walls of King Herod the Great like a waterfall of black sludge as the monstrous demonic foul could sense and taste death in the air. The demonic minions of Satan began a relentless, cruel, and merciless attack upon the soul of Herod the Great. He had sold his now worthless soul to Satan many years ago and now it was time for the devil to collect his payment in blood. His body was now covered with open soars running with a thick yellow puss. The putrid odor from his rotting flesh was so intense that even lavender could not cover up the horrible smell in the palace. As the warmth of his body ebbed, it convulsed in violent trembling as it shook with shivering. The great king no longer could sleep as the demonic spirits tortured his mind day and night as he envisioned massive beasts and hulking warriors trying to assassinate him. Swords, axes, arrows, knives and containers of poison charged his waking eyes yet he would not die only to relive the haunting fear of death over again and again.

Then all of a sudden the great black beast known as the Vulture of Death let out a blood-curdling scream that pierced the ear drums of the evil dark forces and King Herod. At that instant, Herodes (Herod) the Great saw that he had been derided and jeered at by the Oriental magicians from the East and he became much enraged like an uncontrollable madman. So he ordered and sent out on a mission his palace soldiers to become human butchers and he ruthlessly murdered all the boys in Beyth Lechem (Bethlehem) and in all its surrounding regions from two years in age and downwards according to the space of time which he had previously ascertained on the account of the Oriental magicians from the East. The slashing of small and helpless throats and bloody beheadings covered the area in the blood of innocent male children. Their lifeless bodies were tossed to the ground and trampled upon like human excrement. The helpless cries of frightened children and agonizing heart-wrenching screams of mothers filled the air as their infants and toddlers were ripped away from their protective breasts and barbarically butchered right before their tearful eyes. The valiant fathers were outnumbered and brutally beaten by the soldiers of King Herod as they tried to protect their young.

At that time what was uttered and spoken nearly six hundred years earlier by the inspired prophet Yirmyah (Jeremiah) was verified by the prediction as he had said in chapter 31:15 of his book, *"**A tone was heard in Ramah, wailing, lamentations and much moaning. It is Rachel the wife of Yisra'Yah (Israel) sobbing and wailing aloud for her children and she did not wish to be consoled because they are not any longer.**"* Satan began to celebrate his apparent victory. The promised New King was dead and the Sunrise that had been promised by Yahuah to forever pierce the kingdom of the dark lord would never shine again. The Prince of Darkness could now rule the world in the blackness of doubt, fear and ultimately disobedience to Yahuah.

However, there was still one item of unfinished business at hand before the dark lord could think too far into the future. He needed to collect on the bargain that he had made forty-six years ago with a certain young man from the country of Edom. Satan promised this young man that he would make him one of the greatest kings in history if only he would worship him as a god. The young man could not resist such an offer and power and riches became his to enjoy. Now this young man is seventy years old, sick and dying with hatred raging in his tormented soul. King Herod the Great ordered a large golden eagle, the symbol of Roman Rule, be placed over the Temple entrance to signify that even Yahuah was subject to the rule of Caesar Augustus, the self-proclaimed god of the world. This act of flagrant blasphemy infuriated the Hebrews of the great city of Yruwshalaim (Jerusalem) and the priesthood of the Pharisees and Sadducees of the Sanhedrin.

Herod Archelaus, the oldest son of King Herod the Great, quickly sent the royal family and the dying king to Yriychow (Jericho) for protection due to the uprising of the priests and citizens. "Butcher King", King Herod the Great, was very pleased with himself with the last actions of his dying days. He had ruthlessly slaughtered innocent infant Hebrew boys in his quest to kill the "New King" spoken of by the Oriental Magicians from Babel (Babylon, modern Iraq). He also had insulted and caused chaos amongst every Hebrew under his rule by putting their god Yahuah under the subjection of the rule of the throne in Rome. But now, his body of rotting putrid flesh with the mind of a madman had been removed from his palace in the great city of Yruwshalaim (Jerusalem) and taken for isolation northwest to the fortified city of Yriychow (Jericho). There he died a few days later at the age of seventy in 4 B.C., all alone under watchful guard away from the riches and power that he had once enjoyed. His spirit departed his ravaged body and he joined his dark lord master in the pits of hell for eternity. King Herod the Great, the butcher king, would forever have a lasting legacy on earth. However, now he would spend eternity as an unappreciated servant in the service of the vilest creature known to the heavens and earth, the dark lord, Satan.

News of Herod's death soon reached Rome and into the ears of his long-time friend and ally Caesar Octavian Augustus who was dealing with family matters of his own. The best friend of Caesar Augustus, Agrippa, had married the daughter of Caesar Augustus, Julia in 21 B.C. This marriage produced two sons, Gaius Caesar and Lucius Caesar, whom Caesar Augustus adopted as his own sons in 17 B.C. Caesar Augustus had sent his two older step sons from his union with Livia, Drusus and Tiberius to subdue the Germanic tribes in the Alps. The two step-sons were never adopted by Caesar Augustus thus could not be an heir to the throne in Rome. Then in 12 B.C. Agrippa died and Caesar Augustus forced his widowed daughter to marry his step-son Tiberius to ensure that one of his descendants would rule Rome. However, in 9 B.C. his stepson Drusus was thrown from a horse in Germany and died from the injuries. Due to his military success Tiberius was made *tribune* of the Roman Senate by his step-father Caesar Octavian Augustus in 6 B.C. Tiberius took his wife, his step-sister Julia, and retired to the Island of Rhodes because of the public attention Caesar Augustus was showing in that year to fourteen year old Gaius Caesar, the oldest son of Julia and Agrippa. With the uncertainty of his own throne of the Roman Empire, Caesar Octavian Augustus is now saddled with the family mess that King Herod created in his own family as a successor to the throne in Yruwshalaim (Jerusalem). Therefore, Caesar Augustus sent word to King Herod's sons, Herod Archelaus, Herod Antipater (Antipas) and half-brother Herod Phillip to appear before him in Rome in ninety days to announce his appointment of a new king.

While the palace was mourning the death of King Herod the Great, that night two teachers and a group of young men chopped down the golden eagle above the entrance to the Temple of Yahuah. News of this act quickly reached the ears of Herod Archelaus, who had the support of the military to be the next king, and he flew into a madman's rage, typical of his dead father. He quickly had the two teachers and forty other youths arrested and imprisoned until the next day. The next morning, the two teachers and forty youths were taken just outside the northern gates of Yruwshalaim (Jerusalem). There he had them stripped naked, bound to large stakes and sacrificed alive like a common animal. First, their skin was pulled and removed from their bodies amidst the agonizing screams of horrid torture and then the victims were burned alive at the stake as the stench of their charred bodies hovered over the great city in a drifting cloud of smoke. Nothing but death seemed to surround the great city and Herod Archelaus knew he needed the support of the populace if he was to be their next king.

Therefore, that afternoon he appeared on a high summit in the Xystrus Market in front of the Temple Mount dressed in white and sat himself on a golden throne. He promised to be gentle and kind to the populace of the city of Yruwshalaim (Jerusalem) by lowering taxes and putting an end to the political prisoners who were considered enemies of his dead father Herod the Great. However, the demeanor of the questioning of the agitated crowd took an unexpected turn of events as they demanded punishment for those of Herod's people who ordered the sacrificial death of the two teachers and the forty youths. They also demanded that Archelaus get rid of *HaGadowl Kohen*, high priest, Eleazar ben Boethus, a member of the Sadducee Party who had been appointed by his father, Herod the Great. They demanded a *HaGadowl Kohen*, high priest, of greater piety and purity. To this last request Herod Archelaus conceded and agreed to the request of the people and publically announced that Eleazar ben Boethus was no longer *HaGadowl Kohen*, high priest and that a fellow member of the Sadducee Party by the name of Yowshuwa (Joshua) ben Sie would replace him. However, Archelaus was becoming very angry at the presumptions of the crowds and asked for moderation. He said to the crowds, "People of the great city of Yruwshalaim (Jerusalem) hear me out! I promise as your next king that all will be well if you will put aside your animosities and be patient until I am confirmed as your next King by Caesar Augustus in Rome." Then he left the market and headed back to the palace to attend a feast that awaited him.

As the sun set in the west and the city was now covered in the darkness of the "night of death" of the day's events, Herod Archelaus left the large and crowded feast with his wealthy and politically powerful friends. They noticed a loud mourning and wailing piercing the air and the coal black darkness of the night sky. They followed the bemoaning sounds to the origin of their source which led straight to the Temple. Archelaus immediately began to worry as people were streaming into the Temple area by the thousands wailing for the loss of the two teachers and forty youths. As the very loud mourning continued the people began escalating their threatening behavior and zealots who promoted the mourning began aggressively procuring recruits for their faction. This sent chills up the spine of Archelaus and he and his friends quickly made a hasty retreat back to the safety of the palace and summoned one of the military generals to take some soldiers and act as a "Tribune in Command of a Cohort" to reason with the seditionists to stop their "innovations" of trying to take the law into their own hands and wait until Archelaus could return from Rome with Caesar.

The general in charge of the delegation made a mistake and tried to force the crowd to comply with the requests of Herod Archelaus by military strength. The crowd had been pushed to their limits of past events and was not going to be pushed around any longer. Fresh on their minds were the slaughter of innocent infant boys in the Beyth

Lechem (Bethlehem) region, the blasphemy of the golden eagle over the Temple entrance and the murder and inhumane sacrifice of the two teachers and forty youths. Enough was enough! The huge crowd of thousands quickly picked up stones and began throwing them at the general, his delegation and the military troops. Most of the one hundred person delegation was killed except escaping death was the general and his two body guards. After the general left the scene the crowd left the dead bodies of the soldiers lay in the Xystrus Market and in front of the Temple area and continued the wailing and mourning for their Hebrew brothers as if nothing had just happened. It was now shortly after midnight when the general reached the palace to inform Herod Archelaus of the stoning of the delegation and his soldiers.

Archelaus grew beat red and through several curses he ordered the entire army within the walls of Yruwshalaim (Jerusalem) to ascend upon the Temple and disperse the crowd by force, killing as many as the soldiers could kill. The army swarmed upon the Temple Mount with mounted patrols and foot soldiers brandishing their steel swords and spears. As the last person was dispersed from the Temple area over three-thousand Hebrew men had been killed and many more severely wounded. A red sun rose in the eastern sky signifying that blood had been spilled the previous night. The great city was deathly still until very early the next morning heralds sent directly from the palace by Herod Archelaus took to the streets and surrounding territories announcing the cancellation of *Pecach,* Passover and *Chag Ha Matstsah Lechem,* the Feast of Unleavened Bread. The entrance to the Temple was blocked and heavily guarded so that no one dared to attempt to enter for worship.

Many devoted Hebrews including Ya'kov Melek'Beyth Aer (James Henry Ayers) the fan maker and his son ten-year old *ben* (son) Chizqiy left the great city of Yruwshalaim (Jerusalem) and headed north to observe their sacred days of worship. Herod Archelaus was also leaving by sailing on a ship headed to Rome to meet with his brothers and Caesar Augustus to see who would be appointed by the Emperor of the Roman Empire as the next king over the territory of Yhuwdah (Judah), the province of the Hebrew people.

5

The royal ship from Yruwshalaim (Jerusalem) arrived safely at the port of Rome and docked to unload its important cargo. The litter for Prince Herod Archelaus was made ready and the prince walked down the plank surrounded by royal palace guards. He entered the exquisite litter carrier and the eight royal Nubian carriers lifted the litter upon their shoulders and began to walk behind the four mounted horseman whose white horses were all decorated in shimmering gold and pranced with excitement. Behind the royal litter were four more mounted horseman and leading in the front were two mounted trumpeters sounding the way for the royal prince. The streets in Rome became infested with a great stirring and clamoring of inquisitive eyes to catch a brief glimpse of this visiting dignitary. His journey to see Caesar Augustus was met will cheer and well-wishers until he reached the doors of Caesar's Great Hall where he abruptly had to meet face to face a group of enemies-his own family. The warmth of the greetings from the docks to these doors quickly gave way to the icy cold stares and shaking of heads from his brothers.

Finally, the great gold plated wooden doors were opened into the Great Hall of Caesar Augustus and two trumpets sounded and the court herald shouted, "Mighty, Emperor of the Roman Empire and the world, Caesar Augustus, I present to you Prince Herod Archelaus, Prince Herod Antipater and Prince Herod Phillip II from your lordship's territory of Yhuwdah (Judah)." Caesar nodded his head and tipped his golden scepter indicating for the visitors to approach his throne. Caesar Augustus was dressed in a pure white toga with golden trimmings and a small interwoven crown of gold braid upon his curly head of hair. Many leaders of the Roman Senate were also present and lined the walkway leading to the massive throne. They applauded the three princes as they made their way to the front of the Great Hall. Standing next to Caesar, to the surprise of at least two of the princes was Nicholaus of Damascus, the long-time confidant of the late King Herod the Great, their father. Prince Antipas (Antipater) glanced at Prince Phillip II with puzzlement and then glanced at Prince Archelaus whose eyes were fixed forward with a smirking smile plastered on his face. Prince Antipas then grew uneasy.

The three princes reached the front of the room with the members of the Roman Senate present gathering behind them. They bowed their heads in humility in front of Caesar to show respect and then Caesar Augustus began to speak. "First, and foremost my honored guests, I want to give you my deepest condolences to you at the loss of your father. He was a great man, king and dependable ally to the throne of Rome. He was a great personal friend of mine and his presence will be deeply missed. Second, I want to extend my warmest hospitality to you and have ordered that your visit to this great city of Rome be enjoyable. Whatever you wish and desire make it known to your personal ambassadors that I have assigned to you and it will be so. Nothing shall be denied to you while you are visiting except the rule of this throne." This brought much laughter from the members of the Roman Senate and the three princes also laughed at Caesar's humor.

However, Caesar Augustus was not one to make a lot of small talk and always got right to business. Therefore, he said, "Now let's get to the business of why you are here visiting the capital of the world. A king is to be selected for the territory of Yhuwdah (Judah) to rule as a successor to your esteemed father King Herod the Great. These proceedings shall have order and diplomacy. This is the way your father ruled his kingdom and this is the way we shall honor his death and select a successor to his throne in Yhuwdah (Judah). I want each of you to tell me why that selection should be you and I have decided that I will begin with the eldest and finish with the youngest. The order that you were conceived by the deceased king will be the order that you shall speak! However, this is not a trial or a session of the Roman Senate so you will not be allowed to speak out of turn and you will only be allowed to speak once. Do I make myself very clear?" The princes nodded in agreement as Caesar Augustus settled back in his throne and grabbed a chalice of wine from a servant nearby.

Prince Herod Archelaus took half a step forward towards the throne and began, "Oh, mighty Caesar, it is my most humble appreciation and honor that I am able to stand in front of the world's greatest Emperor, a great long-time friend of my dead father and benefactor of the Herod name itself. As the eldest son and legitimate heir to the throne of your long-time friend it is my deepest desire to continue this bond of friendship with Rome and Caesar himself. As a devoted and loyal prince to my father, he entrusted his mighty army to my hands. Thus, I protected and provided security to the interests of my father which were the interests of Rome and even to Caesar, yourself. I carried out his orders without question and without fear of my own life to protect his throne and your direct interests. My father was very dear to me and I mourned with exhausting grief and flowing rivers of salty tears that soaked my beard when the physician announced his death. Why even as I was in deep mourning and heavy distress weighing heavily on my broken heart, I put my own painful feelings aside and personally protected your interests by squashing a revolt by seditionists who were attacking my poor deceased father's architectural legacy of a great golden eagle built in honor of you, oh great Emperor. It was my quick hand that stopped the revolt against your throne and brought swift justice to those who dared to stand against your power and authority in violent defiance and ungrateful appreciation of your generosity towards the territory of Yhuwdah (Judah). I am pleased to report to you that I left the city in a state of peaceful calm before I came to you in Rome. The only logical decision is to appoint me as successor to my father's throne and king of Yhuwdah (Judah). It has the full backing of the entire military might to willingly serve your best interests."

Prince Herod Archelaus took half a step back while bowing his head to Caesar Augustus and Prince Herod Phillip II took half a step forward. He knew as a half-brother it was not wise to get between the blood-brothers Archelaus and Antipas (Antipater). Therefore, he had to maintain an alliance between the both of them to solidify his rightful share of his father's estate. Prince Herod Phillip II smiled at Caesar and began, "My most esteemed potentate Caesar Augustus. Thank you for your warmest and most appreciated hospitality graciously shown to me and my brothers at this most difficult time in our lives. As I was growing up as a young child I will always cherish the memories of sitting on my father's lap in his strong embrace recounting the stories of your friendship with my father. Each time he visited you in Rome I was filled to overflowing with anticipated excitement to hear of the amazing adventures shared with the great Caesar Augustus. My father valued and cherished your friendship more than all the wealth in the royal treasuries. He always told me what wise council that you would give him and the astute wisdom that you provided to your own Roman Senate. Both of my fellow brothers have legitimate claims to be king of your territory of Yhuwdah (Judah). My father would not want a divided house but rather a united throne. Therefore, we can present our cases to you in the most eloquent speech but in the end our father, your devoted long-time friend has chosen to leave this monumental decision based upon your keen wisdom alone. Just know this, magnificent ruler, if I am chosen as successor I will continue my father's historical record of seeking your wisdom of council in dealing with matters based upon the best interests of your throne and supporting your Empire. However, if I am not chosen then also know this. I will be in full support of whichever brother you choose as the next king as long as he is loyal to your throne."

Prince Herod Phillip II took half a step backward while bowing his head to Caesar Augustus and Prince Herod Antipas (Antipater) took half a step forward. Caesar took a long sip of wine, while studying Antipas and then said, "You may begin." Prince Antipas stretched his arms forward to state his case, "Oh, sovereign master of the world. It is such an honor to stand in front of my father's most trusted friend and wisest ally to carry out his last wishes of his throne." Then Prince Antipas did something not expected, he turned and faced the personally selected members of the Roman Senate that had been invited by Caesar Augustus himself. Then he said, "Also, to those chosen by Caesar himself of the Roman Senate who have graciously appeared today to be witnesses of the strong ties between the wisdom of the Empire's throne and the servitude of the territory of Yhuwdah (Judah). Our historical friendship began with its roots deep within the very working hands of the Roman Senate. To you I also extend my hands in humble appreciation for your confidence in the Herod family. Hail Caesar! Hail Caesar!" Then Senate members quickly began chanting, "Hail Caesar! Hail Caesar!"

Caesar Augustus stood up from his throne and waved towards the Senate members and then he motioned for the crowd to quiet down and he sat down upon his throne once again. Then Antipas turned back around and faced Caesar.

Antipas continued his dialogue, "The greatness of Caesar understood the greatness of my father as I also did. That is why I was kept close to him in his final years and handled the administrative duties for my father and acted under the authority of his signet ring. Herod the Great chose me to be his Commander of Audiences and to sit upon the throne in his stead when he was too ill to attend to the daily affairs of the palace and the kingdom. Make no mistake, my father still ruled with an iron hand from the throne even when he was not present. He remained in command until his final breath was taken. Yet, I sat on his throne in his stead because I knew his mind better than anyone and made decisions based upon what he would do himself in those circumstances. Oh great friend Caesar, you knew my father very well. If I was not able to perform the duties of his throne to his liking, you know that I would have been removed from my position immediately by him. As a matter of fact I believe that it was you who said 'It is better to be Herod's pig than one of his sons.' My life probably would have been forfeited if I did not run his throne his way. I also know as his Chief Administrator that I am listed in his will as the next successor to his throne." This brought some mumbling and light applause from the Roman Senate who had worked closely the past few years with Antipas (Antipater).

Then Antipas continued, "Now as for my brother, Prince Archelaus who has not told Caesar the entire truth. Archelaus has never loved our father as deeply as I have. He merely feigned grief from our father, weeping during the day and then at night became involved in merriment into the early hours of the morning. He has been jealous of my position over him and carried out my orders from the throne as his position of Commander of the Armies only because he feared the retribution of my father if I felt the slightest act of insurrection was apparent in his actions. In his statement to you he painted a picture of a great General Commander but he never had to do battle against a military even a fourth the capability of your Roman Army. Instead his foes have been peasant farmers, and most recently infants and toddlers under the age of two years old. Oh, and the revolt he brags about squelching before arriving in your port was caused by his very own heavy-handedness and threats to the Temple worshippers. Once again his great military conquest that killed three-thousand dead was against unarmed citizens of Yruwshalaim (Jerusalem). Oh great Caesar hear me out and mark my words. The threats against the worshippers in the Temple amounted to threats against Caesar himself because Archelaus acted in every manner as King before such title had been given by Caesar. If he will act in this manner before your decision is made then he will not think twice to do it again and use the military of Yhuwdah (Judah) to rise up in disobedience against the Empire of Rome and the authority of your throne if he is made king."

Prince Herod Antipas (Antipater) did not take half a step backwards when he was finished but rather stood with his eyes fixed upon the eyes of Caesar Augustus. The Roman Senate members began whispering and mumbling in low voices after hearing this information shaking their heads at Prince Herod Archelaus. After a long awkward pause, Caesar raised his golden scepter to once again quiet the crowd. Then he put the point of the golden scepter against the arm of Nicholaus of Damascus who was standing on the right side of the throne. Caesar Augustus then said, "Roman Senate members and Royal Princes we have not heard all the facts yet!"

Then Caesar said, *"Ab origine absit invidia ad honorem Herod the Great, Aquila non capit muscas asinus asinum fricat. Auctoritas non veritas facit legem, audi, vide, tace!* (From the source, let ill will be absent, to the honor of Herod the Great. An eagle doesn't catch flies and the jackass rubs the jackass. Authority, not truth makes law. Hear, see and be silent!). Nicholaus of Damascus what light can you share upon this matter?" Nicholaus stared at the stunned crowd and princes and said, "Honorable Roman Senate members I must introduce myself to you as the princes already know me. I am Nicholaus of Damascus, King Herod the Great's only confidant for many years now. I must make it perfectly clear to you and Caesar Augustus himself that Archelaus acted appropriately as King of Yhuwdah (Judah) because King Herod changed his will which was written several weeks prior to his death yielding the Kingship to Prince Archelaus and against Prince Antipas (Antipater). I have in my possession the legal document and it should be seen as valid. The change of his will in favor of Prince Archelaus is given as King Herod's true choice and was written while King Herod was in his right mind since he had left the final decision to Caesar Augustus. The change of the will was one of the King's last acts and it is attested from the fortified city of Yriychow (Jericho) by the Ptolemy himself, the keeper of Herod's Seal. I know this to be true to fact because the Ptolemy is my very own brother."

At the conclusion of the testimony of Nicholaus of Damascus Prince Archelaus fell at the feet of Caesar Augustus and Caesar raised him up and stated, "Prince Herod Archelaus you are worthy to succeed your deceased father, King Herod the Great." The Great Hall was so silent you could hear a pin drop being in shock of Caesar's announcement. Prince Archelaus kissed the signet ring of Caesar Augustus keeping his head bowed. Caesar rose from his stately throne and stood upright smiling down upon Prince Archelaus as he too came to his feet. All of a sudden Caesar held out his golden scepter towards Prince Archelaus and then brought the golden scepter firmly against his own right shoulder and announced, "It brings me great honor to announce in the memory of my long-time good friend, King Herod the Great, that Caesar Augustus will be the only king in the territory of Yhuwdah (Judah) and I shall divide the territory accordingly. I proclaim and give Prince Herod Archelaus the title of *Ethnarch*, to serve me as the ruler over all the Hebrew people. Also, according to the last will of your deceased father I also appoint you as *Tetrarch* (ruler of a quarter) of Yhuwdah (Judah), Samaria and Idumea (Edom) allotting you the greatest part of the kingdom." The surprised and dumbfounded Prince Archelaus nodded his head and said to Caesar, "Thank-you your Excellency."

Then he pointed his golden scepter towards Prince Herod Phillip II and said, "To you Prince Herod Phillip II, I bequeath to you the title of *Tetrarch* and give you your father's northeast portion of his kingdom. Thus you shall have Iturea (modern south west Syria), Trachonitis (modern northeast Jordan and northern Saudi Arabia), Gaulonitis (modern far western Syria), Paneas (modern northwestern Syria home of Mount Herman) and Aurinitis (modern central Syria)." Prince Phillip II nodded his head in respect and said, "I am grateful for your generosity, High Potentate." Caesar paused for a dramatic moment and after clicking his tongue he commanded, "To the youngest from the loins of one of the greatest kings in history, I grant to you Prince Herod Antipas (Antipater) the title also of *Tetrarch* and give to you the lands of Galilee (modern northern Israel) and Perea the land east of the Yardan (Jordan) River (modern northwestern Jordan). I also offer the protection and the full power of military might of the Roman Army if any of your brothers should rise up against you. In addition I give to you full ownership of the Hasmonaean Palace in the Upper City of Yruwshalaim (Jerusalem) near the bridge to the Royal Porch of the Temple. This is my final decree and each one of you are invited to a large exquisite feast hosted by myself this evening at sundown." Prince Antipas replied, "In honor of your profound wisdom my lord." This brought enthusiastic applause from the Senators who began chanting, "Hail Caesar!"

It took nearly five months but word of the division of the territory of Yhuwdah (Judah) and each division's *Tetrarch* finally reached the country of Mitsrayim (Egypt). Yowceph (Joseph) told Miryam (Mary) of the news that Herod the "Butcher King" was dead and that Prince Herod Archelaus was now *Tetrarch* in the great city of Yruwshalaim (Jerusalem). The good news was that Prince Herod Antipas (Antipater) was now the governing authority in Galilee. Miryam grabbed the hand of Yowceph (Joseph) and said, "Oh, Yowceph that is wonderful news. Grandfather will be pleased that the majority of his business can still be done with Prince Antipas instead of Prince Archelaus." Yowceph put his finger to her lips and replied, "Miryam (Mary) you must be careful. They are no longer princes but are the rulers with the power of Rome behind them. Besides, the most dangerous thing is that they still tout the Herod name and a leopard can't change its spots! Always remember a king cobra remains unpredictable and can still strike your hand and inject its deadly poison into your body no matter how much sweet music you play through the flute!" Miryam looked into his eyes and said, "My, oh my, I think this desert heat is getting to your head. You are becoming quite a philosopher aren't you, my dear?" A little embarrassed Yowceph leaned back and answered, "Miryam, all I am trying to say is that your family, our family will never be safe as long as the Herod name remains in power and is given a blind eye by the

Caesar in Rome. We must pray daily that Yahuah will never remove his hand of protection from us and keep us safe."

A few years later as Yowceph (Joseph) and Miryam (Mary) were in a deep sleep late one evening, a great messenger angel of Yahuah beamed with a bright white light in a dream to Yowceph under the night stars in the desert sands of *Mitsrayim* (Egypt). The messenger of Yahuah laid forth words saying, "Yowceph... Yowceph wake from your sleep, receive near the infant and His mother and travel into the region of Yisra'Yah (Israel). At this time for this reason, those who were seeking and plotting against the life and breath of the half-grown infant have died." So he woke up from his sleep, received near the half grown infant and His mother and came into the region of Yisra'Yah (Israel). But hearing that *Herodes Archelaos* (Herod Archelaus) ruled over Yhuwdah (Judah) instead of *Herodes* (Herod) the Great, his father, he was frightened to go there. So having been given an utterance of a divine intimate oracle by a dream, he decided to retire into the allotment of *Galiylah* (Galilee). Thus having come, he took his family to house permanently in the town called Nazareth.

The young family and Bil'am the faithful donkey were very tired when they reached the outskirts of the little agricultural village of two-hundred people. They had traveled over two-hundred and sixty-five miles during the past thirteen days and now they were only half a mile away from home. Yowceph (Joseph) halted Bil'am the donkey who was carrying Miryam (Mary) and Yahusha the toddler. Yowceph exclaimed, "Look Miryam. Home sweet home, isn't that a sight for sore eyes?" Miryam answered, "*Ken*, Yes! Oh, Yowceph help Yahusha and I down. We want to walk by your side when we enter the town." Yowceph turned around and helped Miryam who was holding Yahusha, down from Bil'am the donkey and then the three wayfarers and the lonely donkey began the last steps of their journey towards their home in Nazareth. It was only about an hour before sunset and the western sky was painted with pinks, lavender and orange hues. The travelers felt energized with each step that they took towards the little village. The dusty street in the distance that separated the town was mostly deserted as shop owners were closing their doors and taking inside their valuable wares. The smell of burning wood permeated the dusk air as wood fires were lit to cook the evening meals.

Yowceph (Joseph) reached down and grabbed the free hand of Miryam (Mary) and held firmly onto her soft and delicate palm and fingers. She looked into his brown eyes and found moisture of happiness forming and a grin through his thick beard beaming his pearl white teeth. Yes, they were almost home and her heart began pounding with excitement inside her chest. Yahusha had been so quiet during the trip but now He was chattering non-stop, squirming and waving his arms wildly. Bil'am the donkey didn't seem to get caught up in the excitement but just plodded along behind his masters with his head drooped down hoping for a fresh bed of yellow wheat straw and a bucket of grain as a reward for his toil and faithfulness.

Yownathan ben Yow'ash (Jonathan son of Joash) was always the last merchant to take his wares inside because he was the candle maker and it seemed as if no one thought about candles until the very last moment as it was getting dark. He looked to the north and the dusty street was barren then he took a deep sigh and looked down the street to the south and travelers were approaching. He put his hand above his eyebrows and peered into the distance to get a good look at the travelers. They weren't carrying much so they would have to purchase some candles for the evening. Yownathan ben Yow'ash yelled back to Tamar his wife to let her know that he would be in as soon as he finished with the last customers who were just coming into the village. She came out of the house, clearing the dust from her apron and putting her hand over her eyebrows to get a better look also. She began to cluck her tongue and poked Yownathan ben Yow'ash in the ribs and said, "Go out and meet them. They are covered in white dust and look like they have had a long journey. They might just need a place to stay and a warm meal. It looks like they have a wee one with them also." He began to walk down the dusty street towards the travelers and when he got half way there he stopped dead in his tracks, took a good look and then began waving his arms like a wild man, whistling and dancing in the street at the top of his lungs. Tamar then rushed to her husband to see what was wrong and she dropped down to her knees in the middle of the dusty street lifting her arms and giving praise to Yahuah. They made such a ruckus that Matityahu ben Levi opened his front door to see what the alarm was all about. Tamar began pointing down the dusty street and he………..

6

…..could hardly believe his own eyes. In a short distance coming down the dusty street less than fifty yards from his house was Yowceph (Joseph), Miryam (Mary) and little Yahusha holding tightly onto her hand. Matityahu ben Levi bolted from his wooden front door and ran past Tamar and her husband Yownathan ben Yow'ash to welcome his much loved and missed family back home. By now a few other houses were opening their doors into the dim light of the sunset to see what all the excitement was about. A small crowd gathered in the middle of the dusty street of the little agricultural village of two-hundred people called Nazareth. They witnessed Matityahu ben Levi embrace the young family sobbing on their necks and shoulders as warm salty tears freely ran down his beard-covered cheeks like spring-time rivers. The good news quickly spread throughout the little village like a raging inferno in a dry forest. Soon cook, *Qatan Yow* (Little Joe) and Shalowmit (Salome) emerged from the house and joined the rest of the family in the street. Then spontaneously the crowd in the middle of the street began clapping, singing and dancing.

The crowd soon swelled and swallowed up the rejoicing family and they too joined in the celebration festivities. Matityahu ben Levi danced with little Yahusha on his shoulders as Yowceph and Miryam were busy accepting congratulatory handshakes and welcoming cheek kisses from their friends and neighbors. Cook and *Qatan Yow* (Little Joe) kicked up their heels in the round dancing while Shalowmit had her eyes on a certain fisherman. Now the sun had completely settled behind the western horizon and the street was dark except for the lanterns beaming their flickering yellow lights casting shadows of the townspeople having a great time of celebration. Then one by one as the evening time passed they gradually drifted back to their homes leaving the close-knit family of Matityahu ben Levi all alone in the street. After last hugs and kisses, Matityahu ben Levi, cook, *Qatan Yow* and Shalowmit entered their house and Yowceph took Miryam and sleeping Yahusha across the street to their own house. It was such a great feeling of joy when Yowceph opened the front door.

As Miryam and fast-asleep Yahusha crossed the threshold of the door, Yowceph lifted the flickering lantern and the yellow light shone upon the massive ceiling beams of ruff-cut lumber. On those beams coming to life with the flickering tongues of fire were the scriptural stories of the ancient patriarchs engraved into each beam. The young couple stood there frozen in time as Yowceph wrapped his arm and massive hand around the soft shoulder of Miryam. Standing there together as a family, lost in time, soft and warm tears began to flow from the corners of the beautiful large brown eyes of Miryam and cascade down her brown-skinned cheeks like a gentle spring. Yahusha stirred a little as she held Him tightly to her breasts which brought her back to the present moment and she looked into the proud eyes of Yowceph. Then he said, "Tomorrow, I will begin teaching the characters of the engravings to our Son. Now let's get some rest. This day of the homecoming of our family has been a long hard journey the past two years and now it is time for a *Shabbat* (day of rest)."

The next morning as Yowceph and Miryam were trying to sleep in a little late, they were awakened by a soft tap…tap…tap on the wooden front door. As Miryam let out a groan, Yowceph reluctantly rolled out of bed and made his way to that unwanted noise that had cut their restful sleep short. Each step seemed to make the intrusive noise more repetitive and louder. Within three steps of the door Yowceph barked, "I'm coming! I'm coming! A bird-brained woodpecker is not as annoying as you are!" Yowceph flipped up the latch and opened the wooden door about half way when his sleepy eyes became fully awake to a frightening sight. It was cook pointing her long crooked index finger at his nose with large brown eyes full of fire scolding, "Yowceph it is three hours after sunrise. You may insult me and call me a woodpecker without common sense but it is the bellies of your little family that I am concerned about not your grumpy attitude. Matityahu ben Levi and I know that Miryam has not been to the market yet so Shalowmit and I will have breakfast over here in a quarter of an hour so I suggest that you inform Miryam so that she can prepare a place for all the food. Now, if you really want to ruffle my feathers, then just continue to stand there with your mouth wide open and do nothing! If you are still here when I return, then the next wooden tapping sound you hear will be my finger on that thick wooden skull of yours!" With that said cook dropped her wielding long finger, turned on her heels and marched back across the dusty street to the house of Matityahu ben Levi.

Yowceph in a state of shock watched every step of cook until she closed the front door of the house of Matityahu ben Levi. Then he heard rolling laughter and turned to see Miryam half bent over, holding her stomach and laughing uncontrollably. Toddler Yahusha was by her side, not knowing what was so funny but was also giggling and clapping his little hands together. Yowceph shut the door and muttered a loud, "*Oy vey ist mir* (Woe is me)!" Then realizing what just happened also joined in the laughter. After a few moments, Miryam went into the kitchen still giggling while Yowceph pickup up Yahusha in his arms and gave the toddler a gentle kiss on his soft little cheek. Yowceph half-laughing and half-serious looked at little Yahusha and said, "Never ruffle the feathers of cook. *Ben, ata meiveen otee?* (Son, do you understand me?)" Little Yahusha thinking it was still a funny game clapped his hands together and replied, "*Ken* (Yes)."

The father-son talk was soon interrupted by a rap, rap, rap on the wooden door. Yowceph put little Yahusha down on his own two feet and went and answered the door. When he opened it, there stood cook and Shalowmit loaded down like merchant camels with several woven baskets of aromatic food in their arms. Just as cook stepped inside the house little Yahusha began clapping his hands and dancing shouting, "*Nakar, nakar…nakar!* (Woodpecker, woodpecker….woodpecker!)" Yowceph quickly shut the wooden door and put the latch in place, turning around just in time to see those large brown eyes of cook shooting darts towards him saying, "*Zeh atah k'mo ab, zeh atah k'mo ben!* (Just as father, just as son!)" Cook continued her journey towards the kitchen muttering to herself as Shalowmit trailed closely behind with a huge smile on her face that showed all her pearl white teeth. Yowceph quickly corralled the enthusiastic and celebrating toddler Yahusha by the hand and took him to the bedroom for a continuation of the father-son talk about cook.

After their little chat, Yowceph and Yahusha reclined at the table where a huge buffet had been prepared by cook with the assistance of Shalowmit. The large breakfast included a bowl of *Hummus* which is a dip of pureed chick peas that was to be eaten with the fresh pita bread sitting next to it. The fresh pita bread was also to be used for the other dips of *Tehina, Labaneh* and *Baba Ghanoui. Tehina* is a thick dip with sesame seeds as its base unlike the popular *Labaneh* which was a dip of homemade yogurt cheese. However, *Baba Ghanoui* dip was the favorite of Yowceph which was made of roasted, pureed eggplant. The pita bread and dips were served with a large bowl of *Shakshouka* which was a scrambled and spiced egg and tomato dish. Adding to the delicious buffet were two side dishes of salads. One was the standard vegetable salad that was the custom of the Hebrew people to eat for breakfast, lunch and dinner and the other was a mixed cheese salad combining cottage and feta cheese with cucumbers, peppers and onions. The final part of the morning meal was the mouth-watering *Rugelach* which means "little horns". These are small pastries made from rich cream cheese dough and filled with various fresh jams, chocolate, honey or nuts.

Yowceph blessed the food and thanked Yahuah for the hard work of cook and Shalowmit for which he was extremely grateful. After the prayer cook excused herself and Shalowmit so that the little family could eat their meal. Yowceph started to get up but cook quickly encouraged him to stay seated and eat his meal with his family. Just as cook reached the door she felt a low embrace around her legs. She look down and it was little toddler Yahusha embracing her who had sprung to his feet and had ran after her. Cook encouragingly said, "Yahusha, I'm not going away. I live across the street. Your mother will bring you to see me." Then with a small innocent voice Yahusha said, "*Lo, nakar. Lo nakar.* (No woodpecker. No woodpecker)." Cook turned around and patted him on the head as she winked her right eye at Yowceph and then clucked her tongue. Then with both hands she gently shooed little Yahusha back to his parents and breakfast. As little Yahusha trotted back to the reclining table of breakfast, cook and Shalowmit closed the wooden door behind them and returned home to prepare to go to the market with Miryam later that morning.

Later that morning Miryam took Yahusha and met cook and Shalowmit and headed to the local marketplace to stock up on provisions. Two year old Yahusha was not impressed with the non-stop cackling conversations of the three ladies in His company at the market but all the bright colors of fabric and the tinkling of the pots and pans stimulated His eyes and ears. His favorite attractions though were the animals for sale. This would bring an instant tug on the hand of Miryam as He would try to pull away to get a much closer look at the quacking ducks, clucking chickens, cooing doves, bleating goats and sheep and of course the occasional whining of little puppies for sale. However, Miryam had a firm grip on His hand and His little feet could not get more than a half-step away from His mother.

After picking up some fresh produce, Shalowmit took off leaving cook and Miryam heading off to the butcher and spice vender by themselves. Astonished, Miryam exclaimed, "My word. Where is she off to in such a hurry?" Cook rolled her large brown eyes and gave a couple of clucks with her tongue and replied, "That sister of yours is off to see that fisherman called Zabdiy ben Yonah (Zebedee son of Jonah). His father owns three fishing boats and supplies the market with fresh fish each day. Your grandfather, Matityahu ben Levi has been talking privately with his father Yonah recently." Miryam thought for a little while then she suggested, "Cook, I think it would be nice to have a little welcome home celebration at grandfather's house tomorrow night. I would like for it to be an intimate family affair of just us and invite Zabdiy and his father and mother. I have a surprise announcement to make." A little astonished cook replied, "Yowceph is not moving you from here is he? You just now came back into our lives!" Miryam stopped walking and grabbed the arm of cook and said, "It does involve a decision that Yowceph and I have made as a family but I can't say another word until the celebration. I hope you understand cook." Cook studied the eyes of Miryam for a brief moment then she clucked her tongue scolding, "I just don't like it and your grandfather will be disappointed I hope you know. This will probably break his aging heart seeing your little family leave this village again." Then the two ladies continued their shopping with little Yahusha tagging along.

The next morning, Miryam left Yahusha with Yowceph while she went across the street to her grandfather's house to help cook and Shalowmit prepare for the welcome home celebration to be held that night. Yowceph spent the time with Yahusha teaching Him about all the carvings on the large ruff brown wooden beams of the front room. Yahusha was a very bright little boy and quickly learned the story of Adam and Eve and His love for animals captivated His little mind as He could recount the story of Noach (Noah) and the Ark of the Great Flood. Of course, His rendition of the story was much more exciting than that of His father Yowceph because little Yahusha would add animal sounds as they boarded the Ark. Miryam came home and fixed a quick lunch and then after they ate she took little Yahusha with her to Matityahu ben Levi's to finish getting ready for the celebration and to put little Yahusha down for a long overdue nap. Meanwhile Yowceph went down to the market to look at a sticking drawer on the spice cabinet that he had made for the spice maker two years ago.

The evening celebration finally arrived and the guests were greeted and welcomed warmly to the home of Matityahu ben Levi. Joining Matityahu ben Levi for the feast were the guests Yonah and his wife and their son Zabdiy, along with the family members, *Qatan Yow* (Little Joe), Shalowmit, Yowceph, Miryam and toddler Yahusha. Cook remained busy clapping her hands, pointing and shouting orders to the servants serving the food and tending to the needs of those greatly enjoying her culinary talents and labors. Shalowmit and Zabdiy glanced at each other throughout the meal more than they did at their plates. This did not go unnoticed by Miryam and definitely caught the sharp eyes of Matityahu ben Levi. As was the custom, the conversation of the men dominated the talking during the meal discussing and debating such topics as business and politics while they tried to solve the world's problems. The women listened patiently and silently as their men blustered with the confidence of their opinions in their fleeting roles as kings of the universe during the meal. When the tide of the conversation had lowered to a crawl and everyone's bellies were full, Miryam stood up to speak.

"I would like to thank our guests for attending this meal tonight and for grandfather Matityahu ben Levi for opening up his home. I wanted to have this celebration as a way of extending my sincere thankfulness of my heart for all the prayers that were lifted up to Yahuah for the safety of our family as we fled and hid in the country of *Mitsrayim* (Egypt). Tonight we give thanksgiving to the faithfulness of Yahuah, Who brought us back home safely to our families. However,…" Miryam paused slightly and looked at cook who was now shooting her ice cold daggers from her big brown eyes. Miryam purposefully inhaled a deep breath before continuing and then said, "I know that we have just arrived back home but I must share with you a very important announcement about a decision that Yowceph and I have made about our little family." This made Yowceph sit up straight as he looked at Miryam with great puzzlement. Matityahu ben Levi with great astonishment looked at Yowceph wondering if he was going to return the little family back to *Mitsrayim* (Egypt) or some other far off place. Miryam surveyed the puzzled and anxious eyes of all those at the meal while carefully avoiding the ice-cold stares from cook standing directly behind Matityahu ben Levi with her arms tightly folded across her chest. Then Miryam continued with her announcement, "This decision that my husband and I have made together has forever changed our little family. You see, I am pleased to announce with the full support of my husband that I am with child again!"

The room burst into joyful clapping as the men rushed upon Yowceph and the women gathered around Miryam. Cook stood frozen with her mouth wide open as she tried to process this exciting news because it was far different than what she was expecting to hear. However, the shock quickly wore off and she ran to Miryam with both of her arms wide open like a bull in a china closet oblivious to anything in her path. After a period of time, Yowceph finally made his way to his wife, Miryam and after a long embrace in his arms, he gave her a kiss on the forehead as his eyes beamed with joy. Even though this was the second child that Miryam was to bear, it was the first child of Yowceph and Miryam together. Little Yahusha did not fully understand what was going on but He was giggling, jumping up and down while clapping His little hands together with joy.

Matityahu ben Levi held up his arms and asked everyone for their attention. Order and silence was soon restored with all eyes directed towards Matityahu ben Levi. With a broad smile appearing beneath his aging beard showing off his teeth, Matityahu ben Levi began to speak, "My beloved family and honored guests, the glad tidings of another great-grandchild brings immense joy to this old man's heart. There are two things that fill an old man's heart with such joy. The first, is the announcement and birth of another child being added to the legacy of his linage. Tonight I can honestly announce to you that my heart is overflowing with such joy that my spirit could jump right out of the old and withered skin of my body. Once again congratulations to Yowceph and my granddaughter Miryam for filling this old man's heart with joy tonight. However, my heart is not just full it is overflowing and running over with joy. You see, I said that there were two things that fill an old man's heart with such joy. I have told you of the first but not of the second. The second thing that fills an old man's heart with such joy is a marriage.

For this reason, I must say to all of you once again that my heart is not just full but is overflowing and running over with joy. I am pleased to announce that Yonah and I have come to terms today and the *ketubbah* (marriage contract) has been signed by Zabdiy for the marriage and union of my granddaughter Shalowmit. The *chuppah* (sexual consummation) will take place at the end of eight months from tonight's joyous occasion."

The house of Matityahu ben Levi was once again filled with clapping, congratulatory celebration and finally festive dancing. Never before and never again would this level of abundant joy fill the home of Matityahu ben Levi. The celebration lasted long into the early morning hours of the night sky as even the shimmering stars seemed to dance with joy. Pitchers of fermented wine continued to flow with their intoxicating juice and cook kept the food coming as the guests and family members snacked throughout the evening of festivities. The celebrations eventually subsided and the last person crossed over the threshold of the wooded door to head to their own home. It was Miryam and she kissed her grandfather on both cheeks simply saying, "I love you."

The next year of 1 BC seemed to come quickly as the little community of Nazareth anxiously awaited the birth of the baby of Yowceph and Miryam. In addition all the details of the wedding for Shalowmit were being finalized. These two major events for the family of Matityahu ben Levi kept the town marketplace buzzing with gossip and thriving with drama. It was good business for the local merchants as the women made excuses to go to the marketplace to find out the latest happenings at the well-known household of Matityahu ben Levi. Small purchases of this and that were made of unnecessary things just so the women did not go back to their homes empty handed. Of course, at the most convenient and opportune times the women were quick to fill their husband's ears full of their approval or disapproval of the details of the day's gossip concerning the birth and wedding. The activities, real and unreal, of the household of Matityahu ben Levi consumed the entire village.

Miryam was busy tending to the activities of a housewife and mother after the mid-day meal, when all of a sudden she felt her water break. Yowceph was tossing little Yahusha in the air making Him giggle non-stop while begging for more launches. Miryam calmly sat down and said to Yowceph, "Yowceph it is time. Go get cook. The baby is on the way." Yowceph not questioning kept ahold of little Yahusha and quickly ran across the dusty street to the house of Matityahu ben Levi to get cook. Matityahu ben Levi answered the door and quickly summoned cook. Little Yahusha was left with His fourteen-year-old great uncle, *Qatan Yow* (Little Joe) for babysitting duty and Yowceph and grandfather Matityahu ben Levi went back across the street to patiently wait the birth inside the house. Of course the bustling across the street between the two families did not go unnoticed by the local female gossip spies. The news spread like a wildfire in tall dry grass and soon several people gathered just outside the home of Yowceph and Miryam waiting for the proud papa to come out and announce the birth of the new baby.

Finally, the moment had arrived. The wooden door of the house of Yowceph opened and he stepped outside to cheers and whistles of the anxious and curious crowd that had gathered. Yowceph beamed from ear to ear as his white teeth glistened behind his black beard. As soon as the crowd became somewhat quiet Yowceph announced, "Friends, neighbors and fellow townsfolk. I am pleased to announce to you that today to the house of Yowceph ben Ya'aqob (Joseph son of Jacob) has been born a healthy son." The news brought more loud cheers, whistles and shrills from all those gathered for the occasion. Spontaneous dancing quickly broke out in the dusty street and Yowceph was engulfed with handshakes, kisses on the cheeks and slaps on the back. *Qatan Yow* (Little Joe) had snuck out of the house of Matityahu ben Levi and was in the back of the crowd with little Yahusha on his shoulders when the announcement was made. He cried out, "Did you hear that little Yahusha, you have a little brother." Yahusha giggled as He was twirled around on the shoulders of *Qatan Yow* (Little Joe) and bounced up and down as they joined in the dancing in the dusty street. Eight days later the *brit milah* (circumcision) was held and Yowceph held up his son and announced, "This is my son and I present to you, Ya'kov ben Yowceph (James son of Joseph)."

Three weeks later, the town was buzzing once again as it was time for the wedding celebration of Shalowmit (Salome) the sister of Miryam (Mary) to the fisherman Zabdiy ben Yonah (Zabedee son of Jonah). Zabdiy presented Matityahu ben Levi with the money dowry as was set forth in *ketubbah* (marriage contract). Matityahu ben Levi along with Yowceph as a witness counted and verified the *ketubbah* dowry and then Zabdiy was led to the *chuppah* room by cook where Shalowmit was waiting. After the consummation of the marriage Zabdiy and Shalowmit handed the bloodied *chuppah* cloth "proof of virginity cloth" to the witnesses chosen by Matityahu ben Levi. Then the bride and groom followed by their families exited the door of the home of Matityahu ben Levi and led the procession of the large crowd that had gathered to the wedding feast that had been prepared for this joyous occasion. An abundance of feasting, drinking and dancing took place for the celebration. The next day after the wedding feast the bride and groom left for the town of *Beth-tsaida* (Bethsaida) meaning "house of fishing" to make it their home.

7

Two years later in 1 A.D. the little village of Nazareth was buzzing once again. Miryam gave birth to her third child. This time it was a beautiful baby girl named *Hadaccah* (Hadassah) meaning 'the myrtle' because of her beauty, sweet smell and loving disposition. Proud as peacocks were Yowceph, her father, along with her big brothers five year-old Yahusha and two year-old Ya'kov (James). Of course it went without saying that her eighty-seven year old great-grandfather Matityahu ben Levi gloated and fussed over her as if she was his own pride and joy. Two months later Matityahu ben Levi held another new addition to the family on his aging lap as Zabdiy ben Yonah and Shalowmit a month after Miryam and Yowceph had given birth also gave birth to a son that year in the town of *Beth-tsaida* (Bethsaida) and named him Ya'kov ben Zabdiy (James son of Zebedee). This Hebrew family celebrated with joy and praise.

The days in the territory of Yhuwdah (Judah} were filled with happiness and cheer but in the world capital of Rome blackness and despair loomed greatly. Satan's dark minions drooled with poison and evil and sank their fangs into the ruling government of the world as often as they could. The house of Caesar Augustus filled with idolatry became easy prey to the dark lord Satan. The black cauldron of the dark lord spewed and belched pitch black smoke filled with the chocking stench of death and destruction. The power of the world seemed to be in the hand of the great dark lord to do his bidding in his quest to be master of the universe. The earth was ripe for picking. All he had to do now was to put the finishing touches on the power of this globe and the world would be his to claim as his own kingdom. Nothing could stop him now, not even Yahuah the Creator.

In 2 A.D. Caesar Augustus allowed Tiberius to return to Rome from Rhodes where he had retired against the wishes of Augustus. This also prompted Augustus to banish his daughter Julia, the ex-wife of Tiberius, to an Island off the coast of Italy because of the reputation of her notorious promiscuity. Caesar Augustus referred to his daughter Julia as "a disease of my flesh". In 4 A.D. the dark lord continued to inflict unmerciful calamity and tragedy upon the household of Caesar Augustus. One calm mid-afternoon day, a squire rode feverously towards the palace of Caesar carrying a dispatch in his belt. The palace guards quickly searched him as they recognized that he was the trusted squire of Gaius Caesar, the oldest adopted son of Caesar Augustus. The young lad was quickly ushered in to the throne room and he knelt down on one knee and lowered his head as he said, "Hail Caesar!" Caesar Augustus acknowledged the squire and said, "What news do have for your Caesar?" The squire stood and handed Augustus the scroll as he explained his presence, "I stand before Caesar bearing you grave news of Gaius Caesar from the eastern provinces of your Empire in Armenia. With great sympathy and pain I must inform Caesar Augustus that his son, Gaius Caesar has died in Armenia at the age of twenty-four." Caesar Augustus lowered his head and began to weep as the young squire backed out of the room with his head bowed in respect. Augustus sat motionless in his throne for quite some time mourning the loss of the appointed heir to his empire. What was he to do now that his lineage was spent and gone?

After an evening of mourning the loss of his adopted son,

sixty-seven year old Caesar Augustus the next day held court in the throne room and officially adopted his forty-two year old step-son Tiberius as his son and heir to the throne of Caesar. Immediately following the adoption, Caesar Augustus conferred the powers of the throne of the Roman Empire upon Tiberius nearly equal to his own. With the power of the throne in his hand, Tiberius a week later officially adopted Germanicus Julius Caesar, the son of his dead brother Drusus. This pleased his great-uncle Caesar Augustus very much insuring a bloodline legacy to the throne in Rome.

The bloodline of Yowceph (Joseph) and Miryam (Mary) also expanded that year as Miryam had her fourth child. This bundle of joy had his father's features especially his large hands. Therefore, eight days later on a sunny day in the little village of Nazareth, Yowceph named his new son Yowceph ben Yowceph (Joseph son of Joseph). Even though Matityahu ben Levi was aging rapidly, he still enjoyed blessing his great-grandchildren and required a large celebration to take place. Most of the family business was now being overseen by Yowceph ben Matityahu (Joseph son of Matthew), also known by his family as Uncle *Qatan Yow* (Little Joe) since he was now twenty years old. Land holdings, mining interests and political status kept him very busy. Two years later in 6 A.D. Zabdiy and Shalowmit, the sister of Miryam (Mary) added a second child to their family. The baby was a very robust boy and was named Yowchanan ben Zabdiy (John son of Zebedee). Little Ya'kov (James) now had a baby brother to play with.

This year of 6 A.D. also saw drastic changes take place in the great city of Yruwshalaim (Jerusalem). Rome took over the territory of Yhuwdah (Judah) and Caesar Augustus banished King Herod Archelaus to Vienne in Gaul (France). Now, Yhuwdah, Samaria and Idumea became the Roman province simply known as Yhuwdah.

Therefore, Yhuwdah had its status as a client state removed and now was an expanded Roman province under direct Roman rule. This governmental shakeup also had a drastic effect on the temple powers in the great city. Ananus ben Seth was appointed as new *HaGadowl Kohen,* the High Priest, from the Pharisee party, thus ending the thirty year reign of the Sadducee party. King Herod Antipater, nicknamed Antipas, remained as the Tetrarch or ruler of a quarter, in the territories of Galilee and Perea. Was the black gloom of the dark lord Satan which seemed to control the world capital city of Rome beginning to cast an evil shadow upon Yahuah's territory of Yhuwdah (Judah)? The Hebrew people hoped that Ananus ben Seth as *Kohen,* priest could once again convince Yahuah to extend His covenant blessing upon their nation, His people.

One year later in 7 A.D. Caesar Augustus discovered Agrippa Postumus who was the younger brother of Gaius and Lucius. This discovery threatened the power of the throne now shared with Tiberius. Caesar Augustus quickly disposed of this threat by disowning Agrippa Postumus and banished him secretly to the Island of Pianosa to live out his life in solitary confinement. Caesar Augustus also became very concerned with the limp and slight deafness of Claudius the seventeen year-old son of Drusus, the dead brother of Tiberius. Since Tiberius was hand-picked to assume the throne of Rome upon the death of Caesar Augustus, the Caesar could not allow this handicapped nephew be a stumbling block to his chosen successor. Therefore, Augustus sent Claudius to Livv, which later became known as Lyon, France, to be tutored so that maybe someday he could become part of the royal court of Tiberius without any disgrace upon the royal family.

The evening meal seemed to be ordinary in the household of Yowceph and Miryam with Yahusha age 10, Ya'kov age 8, Hadaccah age 5 and toddler Yowceph age 3. The older children remained silent in the custom of respect to the adults with the occasional giggle while the younger ones interrupted the adult conversation with requests for more food or drink. Tonight's mealtime lesson was on the seven lights of the menorah in the Temple. After Yowceph cleared his throat and washed down the last particles of supper he began the lesson.

"My children and lovely wife the sacred candelabrum with seven branches used for worship in the Most Sacred Place of the Tabernacle is called the *Mnorah* (Menorah). It stands for light, wisdom and Divine inspiration and is beaten out of a solid piece of gold. It stands in the southern part of the Tabernacle and is lit every day by *HaGadowl Kohen,* the High Priest, with only pure fresh olive oil of the highest quality. The *Mnorah* (Menorah) communicates with its unique design as a symbol of the Divine Light of Yahuah spreading throughout the world. Yahuah commanded that the goblets on the *Mnorah,* (Menorah) be turned upside down to emphasize the importance of spreading His light to others. Yahusha, what do the seven lamps represent on the *Mnorah* (Menorah)?" Yahusha answered, "*Ab* (father) they together allude to *da'ath* (knowledge) and the six lamps on the two branches with three lights on each side represent *adam chokmah* (human wisdom)." "Very good and spoken in truth by my *ben* (son)", praised Yowceph.

Yowceph continued the mealtime teaching, "Since Yahuah dictated the creation of the *Mnorah* (Menorah) be made of one hundred percent pure gold, this indicates that we must also strive for "solid gold" with regard to our motives and behavior. What does that mean to you, Ya'kov (James)?" Ya'kov put his index finger of his right hand to his lips and scrunched his eyebrows together as he thought hard contemplating his answer. Finally, his little eight-year old eyes brightened up and he carefully chose his words with the requested answer. "I think that means, that our shining character traits on the inside should reflect the holy actions we take on the outside!" Yowceph clapped his hands together and exclaimed, "Very well said Ya'kov! The *Mnorah* (Menorah) teaches us to bring out every *nshamah* (breath) of our inner Divine light so that we shine internally and externally. Its solid gold composition inspires us to embrace total holiness as we offer ourselves as earthly representations as pure vessels of the light of Yahuah. This concludes tonight's meal."

Miryam was quick to jump right in the conversation as the children began to get up from reclining at the supper table, "Not so fast children. I have something to add to the teaching tonight. You see my dear husband, you don't know this but you left out a major point in your teaching tonight. You see my dear Yowceph, you are going to add another candlestick branch to our family's *Mnorah* (Menorah)." Five year-old Hadaccah exclaimed, "*Ab* (father)! Yahuah will be mad at you for changing His light!" Yowceph and Miryam laughed as Yowceph got up and picked up Hadaccah while tickling her. This sent everyone into chaotic laughter. Then Miryam explained, "*Lo* (no) my *bath* (daughter). Your *ab* (father) is not changing the *Mnorah* (Menorah) in the tabernacle. You are going to have another little brother or sister." Then everyone including little three-year old Yowceph began clapping, singing and dancing around the room. Then late that year of 7 AD, Miryam gave birth to her fifth child, a beautiful girl with jet black hair. She was named Ruwth (Ruth) meaning 'female friend'. This brought great joy to the now feeble Matityahu ben Levi, the grandfather of Miryam.

The spring of the following year not only brought great beauty and life to the vegetation of the Middle-East but it also brought great sadness to the little farming village of Nazareth. The aged ninety-four year old Matityahu ben Levi breathed his last breath on earth. This tragic event in 8 AD ripped at the tender hearts of his granddaughters Miryam and Shalowmit and his son Yowceph ben Matityahu (Joseph son of Matthew), also known by his family as Uncle *Qatan Yow* (Little Joe). However, now that Yowceph ben Matityahu was now twenty-three years old he was more commonly known as Yowceph of Arimathea, where he now lived and controlled the family estates. Since Yowceph resided at the Estates of Arimathea, he had Yowceph and Miryam and their children move in across the street with cook where she could help Miryam with the children. The former home of Yowceph and Miryam then became a guest house and an expanded carpenter shop.

In the spring of the next year 9 AD, the family of Yowceph and Miryam along with many neighbors and friends made the annual trip to the great city of Yruwshalaim (Jerusalem) to celebrate *Chag Ha Pecach* (Feast of the Passover) and *Chag Ha Matstsah Lechem* (Feast of the Unleavened Bread). Therefore, when Yahusha was twelve years old they went up to Yruwshalaim (Jerusalem) according to the law of the festival. While in Yruwshalaim (Jerusalem) the family of Yowceph and Miryam stayed with the fan maker Ya'kov Melek' Beyth Aer (James Henry Ayers) in the Upper City. He was a very dear family friend of Miryam's deceased grandfather Matityahu ben Levi and Chizqiy Aer (Charles Ayers), his son, was the best friend of her uncle, Yowceph of Arimathea. This year Chizqiy Aer had a surprise for the family of Yowceph and Miryam as he had recently become the proud father of a *ben* (son), Ya'kov Gammed Aer (James Walter Ayers) meaning 'the one who overthrows a warrior's breath'. Twelve year old Yahusha spent every afternoon at the Temple listening and questioning the rabbi's about the Torah Law and spiritual matters.

After fulfilling the required days, the family of Yowceph and

Miryam was returning home to Nazareth but the boy Yauhsha remained in the great city of Yruwshalaim (Jerusalem). Yowceph and his mother did not know it but regarded Him to be in the companionship of the caravan on the journey. They had gone a day on the road and began to look for Him among the relatives and the friends but did not find Him. So they returned to Yruwshalaim seeking to find Him. It came to be after three days they found Him in the Temple, sitting down in the middle of the instructors, even hearing them and inquiring of them. All those hearing Him were put out of their wits and were astounded at His intelligence and His responses in regards to the Torah Law. When His parents saw Him they were struck with astonishment and His mother said to Him, "Child, why did You do this to us? Your father and I were grieved and were seeking You." Yahusha said to them, "Why was it that you were seeking Me? Did you not know that I must be about the affairs of My Father?" But they did not comprehend the utterance which He had spoken to them. Then He descended with them and came to Nazareth and obeyed them. His mother watched thoroughly all these utterances in her heart of feelings and thoughts. Yahusha advanced and grew in spiritual wisdom and maturity in size and graciousness with Yahuah and human beings.

Also, in that year of 9AD a future Caesar was born. In a small town of Falacrina, Italy Titus Flavius Sapinus 1 and Vespasia Polla had a baby son named Titus Flavius Caesar Vespasianus Augustus on November 17th. The Flavius clan were an equestrian family. That means that they were *nobiltas Romana* (Roman Nobility). These equestrian families made up the three monopolized political powers of: *patricii* (Patricians) the hereditary cast, the *ordo senatorius* (Senatorial Order) and the *ordo equester* (Order of the Knights).

Three years later in 12 AD Rome was all a buzz as Caesar

Augustus publically announced that Tiberius was made equal in powers to him on the throne. Now the stage was set for Tiberius to rule the world and Caesar Augustus would not stop him. Also that year, the great nephew of Tiberius was born on August 31st in Antium, Italy (modern day Anzio and Nettuno). The parents were Germanicus, the adopted son of Tiberius, and his mother was Agrippina the Elder. They named him Gaius Julius Caesar Augustus Germanicus and he was of the Julio-Claudian dynasty. The world capital city of Rome was not the only place experiencing the birth of children that year. Back in the small farming village of Nazareth Miryam gave birth to her 6th child, another son. On the eight day, the day of his *brit milah* (circumcision) Yowceph named his infant son, Shim'own ben Yowceph (Simon son of Joseph).

Then two years later in 14 AD the last child was born to Yowceph and Miryam, another boy. This made the 7th child born by Miryam. Yhuwdah ben Yowceph (Judus son of Joseph) joined his seventeen year-old brother Yahusha, fifteen year-old brother Ya'kov (James), thirteen year-old sister Hadaccah, ten year-old brother Yowceph (Joses/Joseph), seven year-old sister Ruwth (Ruth) and two year-old Shim'own (Simon). Yahusha and Ya'kov spent the daytime hours working with Yowceph in the carpenter shop building small fishing boats and various furniture pieces. In the meantime Hadaccah helped Miryam and the aging cook with the children and the household chores. With the two older boys helping at the carpenter shop, Yowceph continued in the shoes of Matityahu ben Levi and became the spokesperson and leading elder of the village town of Nazareth. Even though he detested politics, Yahuah had blessed Yowceph with the gift of leadership and he used this gift not only publically but also as a key leader in the local synagogue.

That summer in Rome, Caesar Augustus fell very ill and died

on August 19th. A month later on September 17th the Roman Senate designated the deceased Caesar Augustus as a god. The next day, September 18th Tiberius succeeded Augustus as *Principate* (First Citizen) like Augustus but the Roman Senate did not give Caesar Tiberius the title of Emperor like Julius Caesar had. With the entire power of the world in only his hands now, Caesar Tiberius cut off the financial support of his ex-wife Julia who was exiled and she died of malnutrition.

Caesar Tiberius continued to shake things up in Rome the following year in 15 AD by promoting his best friend Lucius Aelius Seianus who was called Sejanus as *Praetorian Perfect*, which was head of the royal bodyguard. He was born in Volsinii, Italy and like Tiberius was of *Equestrian Nobility*. He became an ambitious soldier before assuming the position as head of the bodyguard at age forty-five years old. His political influence with Caesar Tiberius allowed him to introduce reforms which saw the special unit evolve beyond a mere bodyguard into a powerful and influential branch of the government including public security, civil administration and even political intercession including assassinations of political threats to Tiberius.

In the great city of Yruwshalaim (Jerusalem) that very year witnessed the *Sanhedrin* beginning to experience political changes in the Tabernacle in regards to the *HaGadowl Kohen*, (High Priest). A conservative Pharisee by the name of Ishmael ben Fabus became High Priest setting off a chain of political upheaval within the chain of command of the religious sects of the Temple. The following year in 16 AD a less conservative priest was selected as *HaGadowl Kohen*, (High Priest) by the name of Eleazar ben Ananus. He was not concerned with the political influence of the priesthood with Rome so the following year in 17 AD Shim'own ben Camithus was elected by the Sanhedrin as *HaGadowl Kohen* (High Priest).

That same year General Germanicus, who was the adopted

son of Caesar Tiberius from his deceased brother, came back to Rome to celebrate a massive triumph. Caesar Tiberius commanded a huge celebration consisting of parades, parties and prestigious gifts given to the invited visiting dignitaries. However, Shim'own ben Camithus fell ill and was not able to attend the soiree thrown by Caesar Tiberius. This was a great insult to Tiberius and one that he would never forget or forgive.

That small and some would contend miniscule dissention between the throne in the world capital city of Rome and the Tabernacle in the Great City of Yruwshalaim (Jerusalem) appeared to be a small scratch on the flesh but became a cancer-like boil that would fester and change world history to the vanishing point of eternity. Satan the "great schemer" and master of deception sniffed this miniscule situation out and festered it with the fury of hell. The dark lord began to rant and rave stirring up every demon and demonic force within the realm of his pitch-black darkness. "You lazy creatures of hell what do you see and hear going on upon the face of the earth?" Satan barked. An unfortunate minion of the dark lord answered, "Nothing really master. The humans are generally happy, the world government is running smoothly from Rome and all the religious systems seem to be worshiping you. Heck even the "chosen" of Yahuah seem to be more worried about their ill-gotten gain in the Temple rather than battling you, my dark master." Satan became furious and nodded towards the Vulture of Death and in one swift swoop the mammoth black creature devoured the demonic minion in a matter of seconds. Then the dark lord screamed, "Anyone else want to tell me what a happy and joyous time it is on the face of the earth?" All the evil creatures shook in fear and whimpered in terror. Satan then bellowed, "My purpose, which is your purpose is to kill, steal and destroy! So what are you doing here instead of carrying out your master's mission? Now get out there and battle that light and come back victorious with blood on your fangs and claws or don't come back at all!"

Then Satan turned towards his regional commanders and hissed with his forked-tongue, "Commanders it is now time to carry out operation Deafness and Blind Hearts! Take charge of your troops and attack the human race!" At that moment the black cauldron of the dark lord Satan belched a thick black suffocating smoke with the smell of death and decaying flesh. The evil demonic minions flew effortlessly upon the power of the invisible black smoke with their talons extended and their fangs drooling from the anticipated taste of human blood, chaos and misery. The mammoth Vulture of Death brought up the rear as to devour any demonic minion who chose not to engage in the dark lord's commanded bidding. Satan just had to find the light source for restored fellowship between mankind and Yahuah. Where did that bright light go and what had it been doing the past two decades? More importantly if it still existed upon the earth why couldn't he see it? Yahuah was up to something but what was it? Then dark lord Satan screeched towards heaven, "You should have let them die in the Garden when they belonged to me. Their allegiance belongs to me not You. Can't you see that they don't love You? Save Yourself a lot of trouble and give them all to me. You can't want their kind in *Olam Haba*."

18 AD became the beginning of the battle for the human race and their existence in *Olam Haba* (the world to come). The future of mankind depended upon the fate of the obedience of one special person. Who was it and how was that person going to defeat the dark armies of the massive demonic forces? What was the plan of Yahuah and just how could He gain control of the keys to Death and Hades? The demons first attacked.....

8

......the ill unsuspecting *HaGadowl Kohen* (the High Priest) who suddenly without warning went into violent convulsions and foamed at the mouth. His weak body shook with wild tremors and he moaned between deep gurgles of thick fluid oozing from the corners of his snarled mouth. Within hours of the attack upon his body he gasped his last breath and his red blood dripped from the fangs and talons of a multitude of demonic creatures. Sadness and bewilderment filled the halls of the Great Tabernacle in Yruwshalaim (Jerusalem) as stability was threatened with the *Sanhedrin*. Now the priests had the daunting task of electing a new *HaGadowl Kohen*. Did the Pharisee's have enough support and political savvy to control the governing body of the *Yhuwdim* (Jews) or would the Sadducees seize this opportunity to regain the power of the Sacred Temple?

With the putrid taste of death fresh on the lips of the black demonic creatures, they did not hesitate to attack their next victim in the campaign of Deafness and Blind Hearts. The hoard of black wings flapped in rapid succession towards Vienne, Gaul (modern day Vienne, France). Their next assignment was to attack and kill the now disposed forty-one year old ex-King Herod Archelaus. This scheme by the dark lord was to remove any threats for total dominating power of the *Yhuwdim* (Jews) against the controlling world government of Rome and the throne of Caesar Tiberius. Herod Archalaus was enjoying his mid-day meal which included roasted pheasant. While he was cleaning off the drumstick of the golden bird the demonic beasts clamped down hard upon the throat of Archalaus. Herod Archalaus immediately grasped his throat with both hands and tried to yell out. However, to no avail the demonic beasts refused to lessen the grip on his airway but instead tightened their choke hold. Soon Archalaus fell off his lounging pillow in front of the dining table dead from chocking to death on the meat of the fowl. Even though his bodyguards suspected foul play, there was never any evidence to prove their assumptions. Since this evil deed was completed the dark hoard rushed back to Yruwshalaim.

Only a month had passed in 18 AD since the untimely death of *HaGadowl Kohen* (the High Priest) Shim'own ben Camithus and the *Sanhedrin* was called by the senior *kohen's* (priests) of the Pharisee Sect to elect a new *Gadowl Kohen* (High Priest) before the Sadducee Sect could gain momentum. However, they were unaware of the spiritual darkness which surrounded their minds wielding operation Deafness and Blind Hearts of the dark lord Satan. After days of bickering, power-grabbing, and verbal fighting the seventy-member *Sanhedrin* elected a new *Gadowl Kohen* (High Priest). When the dust had cleared the outcome of the election was a big surprise. Instead of electing another conservative or even the popular slightly moderate Pharisee, the Pharisee Sect did come away victorious but a very powerful liberal had been chosen. The thirty-six year old Yowceph ben Caiaphas, the son-in-law of the retired *Gadowl Kohen* (High Priest) Ananus was overwhelmingly elected to the office. Caiaphas and his father-in-law were only concerned about padding their own pockets and increasing the wealth and power of their family. Therefore, when in the presence of wealthy businessmen or priestly allies he would speak boldly against Roman rule looking for a military leader to rise up against Rome. Yet when at political Roman banquets his praise of Roman rule was as smooth as butter.

The claws of the spirit of Deception sank deep between the powers of the two cities.

Caesar Tiberius that same year gave his adopted son General Germanicus a reward for his previous year's military campaign. Caesar made him *Praefectus* (Prefect) of the entire Eastern Roman Empire. Sejanus was also expecting a rise in the administrative ranks of Caesar yet was denied at the hand of his best friend Caesar Tiberius. Instead of a promotion to the administrative ranks Sejanus remained with the title of *Praetorian Prefect* (General of the royal bodyguard) and was given power over nine-thousand troops. His greed and jealously towards General Germanicus began that day with the gradual poisoning of the mind of Caesar Tiberius with the spirit of Deception against General Germanicus.

Now the world stage was all set for the dark lord Satan. He let out a loud hideous sneering laugh and with a big puff of wind blew a large choking stream of the wrenching death-like odorous smoke from his billowing cauldron of demonic evil. Then he screamed towards the heavens, "Yahuah You thought You defeated me and my armies with that painful light all these years but I am back stronger than ever. I will defeat You once and for all this time and then pitiful weak mankind will worship me as the supreme being. Now watch Your people suffer as my minions do their obedient bidding against all earthly human flesh. I am *Satan* (Adversary) to Yahuah and His mankind followers! I come to steal, kill and destroy and shall not be stopped!" Then another loud hideous laugh shook the darkness of the underworld followed by eerie screeching and hissing.

The following year in 19 AD the poison of that evil cloud of smoke covered heavily upon the earth in the spiritual realm. The Hebrew people, referred to in Latin as *Iudaei* (Jews) had become more prominent in the world capital city of Rome. This prominence increased long-simmering resentments amongst the Roman ruling class thus the Roman Senate began pressuring Caesar Tiberius to take action. Therefore, Caesar Tiberius succumbed to that evil cloud of demonic smoke filled with the nagging persistent and demanding voices of the Roman Senators and issued a royal decree and backed it up with all the military might of the Roman army.

The young General Germanicus opposed the powerful Roman Senators and tried to convince his adoptive father, Emperor Tiberius of the troubles throughout the Roman Empire that such action would incite and become a military nightmare. Caesar had heard enough on the subject and commissioned Germanicus to travel back to Syria to squelch any trouble or uprising in the Eastern Empire of Rome. The very next day the royal squire left the palace of Caesar and took to the streets of Rome to cry out the commands of Caesar Tiberius.

The decree was read as follows by the royal squire throughout the city of Rome: "I, Caesar Tiberius, Emperor of the world, issues the following decree which my instructions are to be carried out immediately. First, my military Generals have the right in any province governed by Rome to demand any *Iudae* (Jew) who is of military age to join the Roman Army and serve my throne and the Roman Empire with loyalty. Refusal to do so constitutes a disingenuous act of vilification against the throne and thus against Caesar, himself and such acts will be met with the punishment of immediate death. Second, all *Iudaei* (Jews) residing in Rome have one week to gather or not gather all their belongings and must leave this city. All *Iudaei* (Jews) are banished from the presence of the citizens of Rome and any and all *Iudaei* (Jews) who remain after the generous seven day grace period will be enslaved for life. This decree is dated June 24, 19 AD by my hand, Caesar Tiberius."

General Germanicus was very popular among the common citizenry and the upper military command. The longer he was in Syria the more popular he became even to the point of rumor of him becoming the next Caesar if the throne of Tiberius was to be usurped. When Sejanus heard of this rumor the evil poison of "Deception" flowed freely throughout his veins as the demonic hoard of beasts filled his mind with evil thoughts and voices from the depths of the dark pit of the underworld. The hideous sneering and screeching rang in his ears day and night as he was being transformed to do the bidding of the dark lord in the campaign of Blind Eyes and Hard Hearts. Then on August 1, 19 AD as he was dinning next to Caesar Tiberius at the celebration feast to honor god Augustus, the deceased predecessor of Tiberius. He carefully began to plot and scheme against General Germanicus placing doubt and fear in the mind of Caesar. Over the next sixty days little by little, word by word, sentence by sentence Sejanus dominated the conversations with Caesar Tiberius as he poisoned the mind of the powerful Caesar with insurrection of the throne of Rome as the rising popularity of his once beloved General Germanicus became equal to his own. On October 1, 19 AD Sejanus, *Praetorian Prefect* (General of the royal bodyguard) was summoned to a secret meeting with Caesar Tiberius. Nine days later in a far-away land of Syria, Sejanus carried out the poisoning of General Germanicus commanded by his jealous adoptive father, Caesar Tiberius. On his deathbed, Germanicus asked his friends to avenge his murder and that his wife endure her sorrow bravely so as not the give Tiberius the satisfaction of causing her any grief. Thus on October 10, 19 AD General Germanicus Julius Caesar died of a lethal poisoning at the hands of corrupt "Deception".

Very early in the spring of 20 AD, twenty-three year old Yahusha and his twenty-one year-old brother Ya'kov (James) was helping their father Yowceph in the carpenter shop. They were trying to finish a piece of fine furniture due to be finished by the end of the week while their father instructed their brother sixteen year-old Yowceph ben Yowceph (Joseph son of Joseph) also nicknamed *"Joses"* on the finer use of the wood chisel. Yowceph ben Yowceph was not as skilled in coordination as his two brothers and father as at times he would forget to remove his finger from the top of the chisel before he began to tap it. This would bring laughter from the bellies of his eyeful older brothers and inaudible muttering from his father Yowceph. His *ka'ab* (cry of pain) would bring a response of *"Oy vey ist mir"* (woe is me) as he sucked on his throbbing finger and danced.

Ya'kov (James) shouted, "Father I think the wooden mallet would be better served on his thick head than on the head of the chisel." Yowceph ben Yowceph sent Ya'kov one of those "I will get you later looks". Their father replied, "You just never mind what your brother is doing and help Yahusha get that piece of furniture done!" Ya'kov respectfully complied with a deep sigh, *"Ken, ab."* (Yes, father). Then the woodshop was once filled with the tap, tap, taping of the wooden mallets striking the wood chisels and rasping sound of the handheld wood planer as it would throw very thin pieces of curled wood chips into the air and then spiral down to the dirt floor into a pile of shavings. The carpenter shop wall held many woodworking tools including various sizes of hand axes for chopping, adzes for smoothing wood, many widths and lengths of hand chisels for making groves or inscribing, pull saws for cutting and bow drills for making holes for wooden dowels, leather or cord lashings. Neatly on a shelf were jars of liquid for veneering and varnishing. The shop always had the pleasant smell of cedar and oak. A pile of native acacia wood stood in the far corner and was kept separate for special boxes or projects. Its hard wood and twisted wood grains was perfect for expensive and beautiful pieces.

Even though Yowceph ben Yowceph may not of been gifted with the finest coordination, he was a very gifted artist. His minute and attention to the finest detail made his work absolutely stunning and could not even be matched by his experienced and famous woodcarving father Yowceph. The wooden piece that Yowceph ben Yowceph (Joseph son of Joseph) was working on was a two foot by four foot piece of wood as a special carving. He had envisioned two horses pulling a chariot with no rider which was from the ancient palace of King Shlomoh (Solomon). His father Yowceph would assist in the selection of the perfect tool but the artistic craft was done solely by the hand of Yowceph ben Yowceph.

Even though this project was only in the beginning stages, you could clearly see the figures of the heads of two horses with their ears laid back a little and their bottom lip open. Their eyes were focused and he was so detailed that he had skillfully chiseled in eyelashes. Even the forelock on their foreheads was detailed to look like it was being blown by the wind caused by their galloping. He only had their heads and part of their necks done but even the necks detailed with muscles and majestic manes. Each day the piece of wood seemed to come more alive as the details of the horses transformed from the vision in the mind of Yowceph ben Yowceph to the wooden block brought to life by the careful chiseling and etching of the hands of Yowceph ben Yowceph. It definitely was going to be a prized project when completed and would take many months to do so.

It was now about mid-morning and the temperature was already getting warm. Their second sister Ruwth brought a water jar to quench the growing thirst of the sweating carpenter brothers and father. Ever since her older sister Hadaccah got married three years ago and now had a family of her own it was now the job of Ruwth to tend to the needs of her brothers and help her mother with the younger siblings. She was now thirteen years old and just had her *bat mitzvah* (meaning daughter of commitment) last year and accepted the responsibilities of being an adult. However the task before her now was to see that her thirsty brothers got a cool drink and then return back to the house to begin helping cook and her mother Miryam get the mid-day meal prepared, served and the after meal mess cleaned up to be used again for the evening meal at sunset. After guzzling down several ounces of the cool liquid, her brothers thanked her for the cool water and her father Yowceph gave her a kiss on her forehead before she returned to the house. She was daddy's baby girl and she enjoyed that position.

As the men were wrapping things up before the mid-day meal, father Yowceph said, "Ya'kov come over here for a moment." Ya'kov (James) replied, *"Ken, ab (Yes father)"*. Ya'kov placed his sanding block down next to Yahusha and walked across the shop to his father who was straightening out some leather cords. Yowceph continued, "Ya'kov, next week I think it would be a good idea if you and Yahusha would get started on your wedding furniture. Nine months will pass by rather quickly and we have a small window of opportunity in the business to allow you the time to devote to pleasing your bride." Ya'kov looked down to the floor and shuffled his feet responding, "I know *ab* (father) but I just don't know exactly what she would like." Yowceph (Joseph) paced his firm hand upon the shoulder of Ya'kov and said with a big smile, "Ya'kov, lesson number one from your father about marriage. Never try to outguess your wife because you will be wrong every time. The best thing to do is to give it your best effort and her tender heart will appreciate it even if it is wrong." Ya'kov smiled as if a thousand tons of desert sand had been removed from his shoulders. Ya'kov was about to say something when all of a sudden they could hear the demanding voice of cook from across the street beckoning them to come to lunch. Yowceph threw up his arms and said, "Let's go to lunch boys." They brushed all the wood shavings off each other as they walked across the dusty street towards the house anticipating lunch.

Cook, Miryam and Ruwth finished putting all the food on the table as everyone reclined in their respective positions at the eating table. The table was set with fresh cantaloupe, grapes, *Blintz* (thin egg pancake wrapped around a sweet mixture of farmer's cheese or fruit filling and fried in butter), *cholent* (a slow-cooked stew of meat, potatoes, beans and barley), *kugal* (baked sweet and savory casserole made of potatoes with vegetables and fresh cheese), *pletzel* (unleavened flatbread with savory onion topping) and for dessert *hamantashen* (triangular pastries filled with poppy seed and fruit jams). They were all seated according to age clockwise: Yowceph (Joseph), Miryam (Mary), Yahusha twenty-three, Ya'kov (James) twenty-one, Yowceph ben Yowceph (Joseph) sixteen, Ruwth (Ruth) thirteen, Shim'own (Simon) eight, Yhuwdah (Judas/Jude) three and cook who assisted young Yhuwdah while she ate her own meal. Yowceph gave thanks to Yahuah for the meal and for those who prepared it and said "Halal Yah (Hallelujah)". Then everyone filled their plates and began consuming the savory morsel dishes in front of them.

The typical family mealtime conversation took place until eight year-old Shim'own asked permission to speak. Yowceph gave him permission to speak since he was not an adult so Shim'own reported, "*Ab* (father) I almost got into a fight with that bully Ysha'Yah (Isaiah) today because I said that brother Yahusha was the best Torah reader at Synagogue. He said that his *ab* (father) was but all you ever do is hear him mumble and stammer. I called him a liar and he wanted to fight me but I said *lo* no." Yowceph looked at Shim'own and said, "It is good that you refused to fight because you should only fight to protect your family or property from danger. However, it is not wise to brag and let your pride bring calamity upon yourself." Shim'own looked down at his plate in rebuke and said, "*Ken ab* (Yes father)." Then Yowceph (Joseph) continued, "By the way what stopped you from fighting because you are bigger than Ysha'Yah (Isaiah)?" Shim'own looked back up from his plate and with all seriousness, "His twelve year-old brother Yow'ash (Joash) had his fists clinched." This brought a round of laughter from the table and then Yahusha said to his little brother, "Thank you for the kind words about Me today but it is better to keep you opinions inside yourself unless you are paying a compliment to that person your opinions are intended. A nose kept on your own face is better than bringing a bloodied one home." Yowceph concluded, "A very wise and practical saying Yahusha. A good lesson learned."

They were just about to begin partaking of dessert when all of a sudden there was a ruckus at the edge of the little farming village of Nazareth. Someone was pounding on the front door of their home screaming, "Quick Yowceph, Roman soldiers are coming!" Yowceph and the three oldest boys immediately jumped up from reclining at the table, gathered their cloaks and ran outside to investigate the matter. The Roman Centurion (a roman soldier in charge of one hundred men) instructed his soldiers to gather everyone out of their homes and force them to the town square. Once everyone was gathered the Centurion asked his squire to read the decree enacted by Caesar Tiberius, "I, Caesar Tiberius, Emperor of the world, issues the following decree which my instructions are to be carried out immediately, My military Generals have the right in any province governed by Rome to demand any *Iudae* (Jew) who is of military age to join the Roman Army and serve my throne and the Roman Empire with loyalty. Refusal to do so constitutes a disingenuous act of vilification against the throne and thus against Caesar, himself and such acts will be met with the punishment of immediate death. This decree is dated June 24, 19 AD by my hand, Caesar Tiberius"

Since Yowceph (Joseph) was the chief of the village he spoke up to the Roman Centurion, "Please, sir our young men are not soldiers. They are poor farmers and the others help their fathers operate their small shops to support their families. We pay our taxes and tributes to the throne of Rome and to Caesar every year. Isn't that enough, without taking our sons also?" The Roman Centurion put back on his helmet with the red plume and barked, "Bring that man to me." Two Roman soldiers seized Yowceph by the arms and manhandled him to the Centurion on the horse, who then insisted, "Who is this dung of the earth and by what right do you have to speak to the voice of Rome like that!" Yowceph replied, "I am Yowceph, the chief of the village." At that moment the Centurion nodded towards the soldier who instantly thrust his spear through the mid-section of Yowceph. Then the soldiers took the baker's son, the spice maker's son and the son of a trinket vender leaving Yowceph (Joseph) the husband of Miryam (Mary) dead in a pool of blood on the dusty street.

Three years later in 22 AD, Caesar Tiberius decided to share the power of the throne of Rome with his son Drusus. Therefore, Nero Claudius Drusus with the adopted name of Drusus Julius Caesar received from Caesar Tiberius *tribunicia potestas* (trivunician power), a distinction reserved solely for the emperor or his immediate successor. Despite his violent temper and heavy drinking, Drusus showed promise with both military and politics. He had served nine years as a permanent member of the Senate and heading the committee that drew up the daily business of the Senate. Seven years earlier he had become consul and for three years he served as governor of Illyricum (Yugoslavia). He had been married to Livilla for 18 years but was unaware that she had begun a relationship with Sejanus, the *Praetorian Prefect* (commander of the royal bodyguard) three years ago in 19 AD. The following summer in 23 AD Drusus became suspicious of Sejanus and made no secret of his antipathy towards Sejanus to his father, Caesar Tiberius. Caesar Tiberius refused to cross his long-time friend Sejanus, therefore the operation of the dark lord Satan "Blind Eyes and Hard Hearts" continued to gain strength. Finally, one day during the course of a casual argument between Drusus and Sejanus over administrative protocol. Drusus became instantly angry raised his fist and struck Sejanus in the face, knocking him down to the marble floor of the palace with blood oozing from the corner of his battered lip.

For reasons of self-survival and his own lofty designs of supreme power, Sejanus needed to remove Drusus from the scheme of political power of the Roman throne. Therefore, with the help of the wife of Drusus, Livilla, as the accomplice, Sejanus poisoned Drusus her husband and son of Caesar Tiberius on September 14, 23 AD. Thus the prodigy to the throne of Rome was dead at the age of thirty-four. There was not any suspicion because the evil act giving the Vulture of Death a taste of fresh blood was carried out by the personal cupbearer of Drusus, Lygdus and the personal physician of Livilla, Eudemus. Sejanus as head of the bodyguard made sure that both Lygdus and Eudemus had rock solid alibis and could not be placed at the scene of the murder. Two years later in 25 BC, Sejanus went to his long-time friend Caesar Tiberius and begged him to allow Livilla to marry him but Tiberius became outraged and refused to allow his niece who was also his daughter-in-law to marry Sejanus. What could stop this Death and Deception from the campaign of "Blind Eyes and Hard Hearts" from the evil dark lord Satan and his demonic minions?

9

All seemed well in the demonic underworld lair of the evil and hideous dark lord Satan. Greed and deception were a common practice in the government mechanism of the world capital city of Rome. The government capital of Rome and the spiritual capital of Yruwshalaim (Jerusalem) were at odds with each other. The common *Yehud* (Jew) mistrusted the priesthood because they were oppressed by the Roman soldiers and strong armed military while the *Gadowl Kohen* (High Priest) capitulated to the whims and desires of the representatives of the Roman world government padding their pockets at each transaction. Satan was ecstatic because Yahuah's people were miserable, helpless and hopeless. The giant black-winged monster Vulture of Death flew unchecked sinking its fangs and talons into the helpless and hopeless innocent. The putrid poison of Deception overran the minds of the *Sanhedrin* (the ruling body of seventy priests) as they sought the uprising of a young military warrior that they could crown as king to overthrow the oppression of the Roman military government. The Hebrew scribes combed through the *Torah Law* and the books of the prophets being blinded by the poison of Deception convinced themselves and the *kohen's* (priests) that a military king would rise up from the Davidic lineage and free them from Roman rule and become an independent nation once more. This effort by the blind and hard hearted scribes brought hideous sneering from the dark lord that echoed endlessly off the dark walls of the demonic underworld.

The demonic minions of Satan scurried unchecked across the

face of the earth spreading their putrid poison of disease, despair and ultimately untimely death. The will of mankind seemed to willingly give up a fight for morally right. Selfish ambitions dominated the landscape crushing those in opposition or taking advantage of the less fortunate who happened to be in the wrong place at the wrong time. The evil cauldron of the dark lord Satan timelessly billowed out its thick choking black smoke of death and destruction heavily laced with toxic Deception. Satan had mixed up a perfect brew of sewage in his cooking pot in order to bring mankind into subjection on its knees to worship him as the supreme god. Mankind had every desire the world could offer within its fingertips to tantalize its hard heart. Now all mankind had to do now was close its blind eyes and deaf ears and not only reject its Creator Yahuah but to even forget His Name. Thus hatred, mistrust, selfish greed, self-centered thoughts and self-serving actions dominated the daily life of mankind. No matter how many animals were ritualistically sacrificed on the altars the fellowship between mankind and Yahuah was growing dim as their hearts continuously yearned after worldly desires of idolatrous power, prestige and possessions.

Just as the light of fellowship between mankind and Yahuah was all but snuffed out by the toxic smoke fumes of the evil cauldron of the dark lord Satan a very small flicker of light appeared out of nowhere. It was so small that even went unnoticed by the mass of the swarming hoard of demonic minions. It came out of the hill country to the desert in the spring of 26 AD. Yowchanan ben Zkryah (John son of Zacharias) heard the command of Yahuah. He became known as *Yowchanan Matbyl* (John the Baptist), the second cousin of Yahusha. He began preaching a message of repentance against blind eyes and deaf ears and then submersion baptism as a public act of profession of faith in Yahuah. *Yowchanan Matbyl* (John the Baptist) possessed his apparel of the outer robe made from hairs of a camel and a belt of hide was around his hips. His nourishment was grasshoppers and wild honey.

This took place in the fifteenth year of the official term in government of Caesar Tiberius the Roman Emperor, ruling in Yhuwdah (Judea) was Pontios Pilatos and ruling as the Tetrarch, the governor of a fourth part of province of Galiylah (Galilee) was Herodes (Herod Antipater [Antipas]) and his brother Philippos (Herod Phillip) ruled as Tetrarch of Yruwr and the territory of Trachonitis (the middle region of Syria) and Lusanias ruled as Tetrarch of Abilene, the upper region of Syria. *HaGadowl Kohen* (the High Priest) was Chananyah (Ananus) acting through his son-in-law Kaiaphas (Caiaphas).

Yowchanan Matbyl (John the Baptist), went into all the region around the Yardan River (Jordan River) heralding as a public crier the divine truth of the Gospel through an immersion baptism of a reformation and a reversal of one's decisions for the pardon and freedom of sins as it was written on the inner bark of the papyrus plant made into a scroll of things said by the inspired prophet Ysha'Yah (Isaiah) relating in words in chapter forty verses three through five, **"The sound of his loud voice calling out in the desert pasture, make ready the road of Yahuah. Make straight and even a thoroughfare in the desert pasture for our Yahuah. Every gorge with lofty side will be lifted up and every mountain and hillock will become a level plain and the mountain ridges a wide level valley. The Yahusha** (salvation) **of Yahuah will be revealed and all flesh will see it together for the mouth of Yahuah has spoken."**

Accordingly, *Yowchanan Matbyl* (John the Baptist) said to the Pharisees and Sadducees coming out with the throngs of rabble to be submerged fully wet in baptism by him, "Offspring of poisonous snakes! Who instructed you to run away and vanish away from the upcoming suffering and punishment? Do not trust in your religious ancestry, however good you may think it may be, you must personally have a right relation with Yahuah. Therefore, accordingly make suitable plucked fruit to reversing your decision of being in guilt and do not commence to relate in words among yourselves, 'We possess father Abraham!' For this reason, I relate in words to you as a set discourse that Yahuah is able to produce from out of these stones children of Abraham. Even now the axe is laid outstretched at the root of the trees. Accordingly, every tree that does not make good plucked fruit is being cut down and is being violently thrown into the fire like lightning."

A rug merchant in the throng of rabble inquired of him relating in words, "What then should we do?" *Yowchanan Matbyl* (John the Baptist) responded to them saying, "He possessing two tunic shirts, let him give over to share with those not possessing one. Also, the one possessing food let him do similarly." Others who also came out were tax farmers who collected the public revenue and wanted to be submerged fully wet in baptism said to him, "Instructor, what should we do?" He said to them, "Collect nothing more than what you are prescribed to do." Even those serving in the Roman military inquired of him relating in words, "And what should we do?" *Yowchanan Matbyl* (John the Baptist) instructed, "Do not intimidate or shake thoroughly any man, woman or thing or defraud by extorting and exacting unlawfully and be satisfied with your stipend of rations as a soldier's pay."

The people in the anticipation of hope all reckoned thoroughly and deliberated in their hearts of thoughts and feelings about *Yowchanan Matbyl* (John the Baptist), thinking he might be the Messiah. However, *Yowchanan Matbyl* (John the Baptist) responded to all sternly saying, "In fact, I submerge you to be fully wet in baptism but He that is coming is more forcible than me, of whom I am not fit in character to loosen the ties of His sandals. He will submerge you in the baptism of the Sacred Breath (Holy Spirit) and with fire like lightning! Of whom the winnowing fork is in His hand and He will cleanse perfectly His threshing floor of the grain and chaff. He will collect the wheat into His granary but the chaff He will consume wholly with perpetual fire like lightning that can't be extinguished!" In fact, with many different things by calling near and inviting, he announced the good news of the Gospel to the people.

As a small light was beginning to flicker once again in Yhuwdah (Judah) the dark demonic forces continued to influence the world capital city of Rome with its black poisonous snares during the summer of 26 AD. Caesar Tiberius threw a grand banquet on the first day of July to celebrate the past reign and honor his deceased uncle, the Roman god Julius Caesar. Invited to the party were Tetrarchs Herodes Antipater (Herod Antipas) and his wife Phasaelis, the daughter of King Aretas IV of Nabatea (Arabia) and his brother Philippos (Herod Phillip). Herodes Antipater stayed at the villa of his brother Philippos (Herod Phillip) during the celebration. During this celebration Herodes Antipater fell in love with his sister-in-law Herodias, the granddaughter of the deceased King Herod the Great and current wife of Philippos (Herod Phillip). The two agreed to marry each other as soon as Herodes Antipater could divorce his wife Phasaelis. Caesar Tiberius learned of the affair which could affect half his kingdom in the Eastern Empire. Caesar Tiberius refused to confront Herodes Antipater because Herodes Antipater had constructed a magnificent capital city of Tiberias on the western shore of the Sea of Galilee to honor Caesar Tiberius. Therefore, Tiberius went into exile and put his trusted friend Sejanus the *Praetorian Prefect* (commander of the royal bodyguard) in control of the entire Roman Empire mechanism.

In the autumn of that same year, the family of Miryam met at her house in Nazareth to journey to Yruwshalaim (Jerusalem) for the celebration of *Chag HaCukkah*, the Feast of Tabernacles. Shalowmit and her husband Zabdiy ben Yonah came from *Beth-tsaida* (Bethsaida) with their sons, Ya'kov with his family and Yowchanan. Also joining the caravan were all of her children: twenty-nine year-old Yahusha, twenty-eight year old Ya'kov and his family, twenty-five year old Hadaccah and her family, twenty-two year old Yowceph ben Yowceph and his family, nineteen year-old Ruwth and her family, fourteen year-old Shim'own and nine year-old Yhuwdah. They would stop just north of Yruwshalaim (Jerusalem) to meet Uncle Yowceph in the hill country at the Estate of Arimathea (Ha-ramathaim, known as the ancient city of Ramah) at his business estate, who once had the nickname of *Qatan Yow* (Little Joe). They would stay at his Estate during the celebration since it was only seven miles from the Great City which was about an hour journey from the northern gate of Yruwshalaim (Jerusalem).

Yahusha turned thirty years old on the first day of the celebration of *Chag HaCukkah* (the Feast of Tabernacles). After the seven days of celebrating the Feast of Tabernacles and the one day following feast of *Ha Achariyth Gadowl Yowm* (The Last Great Day) Yahusha decided not to return back home with the caravan of His family but instead went to visit His second cousin, *Yowchanan Matbyl* (John the Baptist) thirty miles east of Yruwshalaim (Jerusalem) on the Yardan River (Jordan River) located just nine miles north of the Dead Sea. Therefore, after arriving from the farming village of Nazareth in the district of *Galiylah* (Galilee) for the feasts in Yruwshalaim He went to the Yardan River (Jordan River) to be baptized by His second cousin.

Yowchanan Matbyl (John the Baptist) was praying and baptizing when Yahusha walked into the water of the Yardan River.

Then Yowchanan recognized his cousin and utterly prohibited Him laying forth words, "I possess a requirement to be submerged fully wet by You! Yet You come to Me?" But Yahusha responded and said to him, "Permit it at this time because in this way it is proper and right for us to verify the prediction of all equity in character and justification." So *Yowchanan Matbyl* (John the Baptist) began praying and did as Yahusha requested and submerged Him to be fully wet. Yahusha being submerged fully wet at once came up from the water. Then the sky of heaven, the abode of eternity, happiness and power of Yahuah was opened up to Yowchanan. He saw the Sacred Breath (Holy Spirit) of Yahuah descending as if it was a pigeon dove and it came upon Yahusha. All at once a thunderous reverberating voice came from out of the heavens and said, "This is My Son, the Beloved, in whom I think well and approve of." *Yowchanan Matbyl* (John the Baptist) kissed the wet bearded face of Yauhsha on both cheeks and Yahusha returned the greeting back to Yowchanan.

Earlier when Yahusha came up from the water and the white pigeon dove descended upon Him a very bright light pierced the darkness of the spiritual realm and sent the evil demonic minions of Satan scampering and screeching back to the darkness of the underworld. Also, the chocking cloud of toxic fumes of the cauldron dissipated into thin air and the fire under the cauldron was extinguished. Then the thunderous reverberating voice of Yahuah shook the demonic underworld of the dark lord Satan with tremors not known to mankind. Spiritual bodies upon black demonic spiritual bodies clamored upon each other in fear of the tremors of the voice of Yahuah and to escape the piercing painful light of the loving restored fellowship from Yahuah to mankind. Satan went into an uncontrollable cursing rage and his red hollow eyes glowed bright red with hatred and anger. His nasty long sharp talon-like fingernails shredded demonic beasts to pieces as he flung wildly his arms throughout his kingdom frantically trying to stop the hasty retreat of his demonic minions.

Then he screamed in a hollow-like and raspy hissing voice, "Yahusha Yahuah I will destroy You and mankind myself! I am the supreme god of this world and *Olam Haba* (world to come)! You will bow before me and worship my presence when I am through with You. Your eternal love for mankind will be Your downfall and will end in defeat for You for which I will take eternal pleasure!" Following this verbal tirade the dark lord Satan commanded in his screeching hollow raspy hissing, "I want all my generals at my side right now and we are off to the face of the earth to destroy Yahusha Yahuah." The military power of the spiritual underworld made haste towards descending upon the face of the earth which had not been seen since the ancient time when Mosheh and Yahuah shook their world with the ten plagues in *Mitsrayim* (Egypt) the night of *Pecach* (Passover), the shedding of blood of the Passover lamb to protect the firstborn from angel of death. They could see Yahusha leaving from the Yardan River (Jordan River) and heading back to the Estate of Arimathea. Just as the dark lord and his generals were ready to descend and attack Yahusha they were met midair by *Miyka'Yah* (Michael) and four large warring messengers of Yahuah with whirling double-edged swords of light. *Miyka'Yah* (Michael) announced in a commanding deep voice, "Satan only you may pass. All others will be destroyed and sent to the arid bottomless pit if they try to follow!" Satan cautiously slid by *Miyka'Yah* (Michael) keeping his penetrating red eyes focused upon the whirling double-edged sword of light held in the right hand of *Mikya'Yah* (Michael).

Just as Yahusha was about to reach the outskirts of the city of *Yriychow* (Jericho) the Sacred Breath of Yahuah (Holy Spirit) led Yahusha up into the lonely wasteland to be tested and enticed by Satan the slanderer. Having abstained from food for forty days and forty nights, eventually He was famished and craved food. Then approaching and coming near Him the enticer Satan hissed, "If you are the Son of Yahuah speak in order that these stones may become loaves of raised bread." However, Yahusha responded, "It has been written, human beings will not solely live on loaves of raised bread but on every utterance proceeding and discharged from the mouth of Yahuah." Then Satan the slanderer received Him near for teaching into the sacred city with walls and stood Him on the top corner of the winglet of the sacred place, the central sanctuary of the Temple of Yruwshalaim (Jerusalem) and cunningly whispered in a hollow voice, "If you are the Son of Yahuah, throw Yourself downwards! For this reason it has been written 'To the messengers of Yahuah He will enjoin around You and they will lift and take You up on their hands lest You stub Your foot or trip up on a stone." Yahusha make His thought known to Satan and spoke to him, "Again, it has been written, 'You must not test thoroughly Yahuah your Yah." Again Satan the slanderer received Him near for teaching to a very lofty mountain and showed Yahusha all the rulers, realms and royalty of the orderly arrangement of the world and their glory. Then the dark lord Satan said to Him, "all of these things I will give to You, if You will fall down and prostrate Yourself in homage, reverence and adoration to me like a dog licking his master's hand." Then Yahusha firmly commanded "Withdraw and sink out of sight Satan you slanderer! For this reason it has been written 'You will only prostrate yourself in homage, reverence and adoration to Yahuah your Yah and you will minister in religious homage to Him only."

Having completed entirely every experiment of adversity, Satan deserted Him until a set and proper time. Immediately messenger angels from Yahuah brought tidings, approached and waited upon Yahusha as menial attendants.

One day near the small town of *Beyth-aniy* (Bethany) located on the eastern slope of *Har HaZeitim* (The Mount of Olives), Yahusha was visiting some old family friends, sisters Martha and Miryam (Mary) and their brother El'azar (Lazarus) whose mother was Aziel. Thirty years ago Aziel gave Yahusha's mother Miryam (Mary) the faithful donkey named Bi'lam when Miryam was carrying Yahusha in her womb. They heard *Yowchanan Matbyl* (John the Baptist) preaching so they moved closer in the middle of the crowd so that they could hear him more clearly. They heard the evidence given by *Yowchanan Matbyl* (John the Baptist) when the *Yhudiy* (Jews) from Yruwshalaim (Jerusalem) sent out on a mission the priests and *Leviyiy* (Levites) that they could interrogate him.

They asked, "Who are you?" *Yowchanan Matbyl* (John the Baptist) did not contradict and assented to acknowledge, "I am not the Anointed Messiah!" Therefore, they interrogated him further, "What then? Are you Eliyah (Elijah)?" He replied quickly, "I am not." So they asked, "Are you the Inspired Prophet?" *Yowchanan Matbyl* (John the Baptist) answered, "*Lo!* (No)" In frustration they said to him, "Who are you under orders that we may give a response to those who dispatched us? What do you say about yourself?" Dressed in his camel haired garment of clothing *Yowchanan Matbyl* (John the Baptist) took a deep breath, waited for silence and said in a loud voice, "I am a voice shouting in a tumultuous way in the desert. Straighten the road of the Anointed Messiah, just as Ysha'Yah (Isaiah) the inspired prophet spoke in his writing." Those having been sent out on a mission with all the questions were out of the *Parash* (Pharisee Sect). They continued to interrogate him asking, "Why then do you submerge to make fully wet in baptism, if you are not the Anointed Messiah or Eliyah (Elijah) or the Inspired Prophet?" *Yowchanan Matbyl* (John the Baptist) growing tired of the interrogation firmly responded to them relating in words, "I submerge to make fully wet in baptism in water. But among you stands One you do not know. It is the One who is coming behind me who has existed in front of my time of whom I do not exist as suitable that I should loosen the straps of His sandals under His feet."

On the next day, *Yowchanan Matbyl* (John the Baptist) saw Yahusha coming towards him and related in words, "Look now! The Lamb of Yahuah lifting and taking away the sins of the world. This is He about whom I said, behind me comes a Man who existed in front of my time because He was first in time and importance. I did not know him but that He be rendered apparent to Yisra'Yah (Israel). Therefore, I came submerging to make fully wet in baptism in water." *Yowchanan Matbyl* (John the Baptist) continued to testify stating, "I have looked closely at the Sacred Breath (Holy Spirit) descending down as a pigeon dove from out of Heaven the eternal abode of Yahuah and He stayed on Him. I did not know Him, but the One dispatching me to submerge to make fully wet in baptism in water that One said to me, 'On whomever you see the Sacred Breath (Holy Spirit) descending down and staying on Him, this is the One baptizing in the Sacred Breath.' I have stared at and have testified as a witness that this is the Son of Yahuah!"

The following day *Yowchanan Matbyl* (John the Baptist) stood again with two of his pupils looking at Yahusha walking and treading all around so he said again, "Look now! The Lamb of Yahuah!" When the two pupils heard him say this, they became united on the same road and followed Yahusha. Yahusha twisted around and looked closely at them accompanying Him so He asked, "What do you seek?" They said to Him, "Rhabbi, (which is expressed in translation as Teacher), where do you stay?" He replied to them, "Come and see." So they cane and saw where He stayed and they stayed with him. It was about the tenth hour that day (4:00 p.m.). Andreas (Andrew) was the brother of Shim'own Kepha (Simon Peter). Andreas (Andrew) also was one of the two hearing what *Yowchanan Matbyl* (John the Baptist) had said and had that day decided to follow Yahusha as a disciple. Andreas (Andrew) first found his own brother, Shim'own (Simon) and expressed to him, "We have found the Anointed Messiah!" Then he led him to Yahusha and Yahusha said, "You are Shim'own ben Yowchanan (Simon the son of John). From now on you shall be called Kepha." (Which translates means piece of the Rock).

The next day Yahusha proposed to return back to *Galiylah* (Galilee). Then He found Philippos (Phillip) and expressed in words to him, "Accompany Me as a disciple!" Philippos (Phillip) was from the fishing village of *Beth-tsaida* (Bethsaida meaning 'house of fisherman') the hometown of Andreas and Kepha (Peter). Philippos quickly went and found his friend Nthane'l (Nathanael) and said to him, "We found whom *Mosheh* (Moses) wrote in the Law and the inspired Prophets, Yahusha from Nazareth!" Nthane'l said to him, "Can anything good exist and come out of Nazareth?" Philippos responded, "Quick, come and see!" Yahusha saw Nthane'l come towards Him so He related about him, "Look now, truly a *Yisra'Yahiy* (Israelite) in whom no trick or decoy does not exist." Nthane'l surprised said, "From where do you know me?" Yahusha responded, "Prior to you being called by Philippos, I saw you under the fig tree." Nthane'l fell to the ground and replied, "Rhabbi You are the Son of Yahuah! You are the Sovereign of Yisra'Yah (Israel)!" Yahusha said to him, "Because I spoke to you that I saw you down under the fig tree, you have faith and entrust your spiritual well-being to the Messiah! Greater things than these you will see! Firmly and surely I relate to you from now on you will see the sky of Heaven, the eternal bode of Yahuah opened up and the messenger angels of Yahuah going up and descending down on the Son of Man!" Then the five of them left the area of Yruwshalaim (Jerusalem) and headed north to the district of *Galiylah* (Galilee).

After three days of travel the small band arrived in the town of *Qanah* (Cana) in the territory of *Galiylah* (Galilee). There was a wedding that day and Miryam (Mary) the mother of Yahusha was there because it was His sister Ruwth's wedding. Yahusha was invited so he brought his four pupils. Being short of wine, the mother of Yahusha expressed to Him, "They do not possess any wine." Yahusha respectfully replied, "Woman what does that have to do between Me and you? My hour has not yet arrived." His mother said to the servants, "Whatever He says to you, do it!" There six stone water jars for the family's water supply standing according to the washing off of the Yhudiy (Jews) each holding two or three measures (thirty gallons). Yahusha said to them, "Fill entirely the water jars of water." So the servants filed them entirely up to the very tops. Then He instructed them, "Now draw out with a pitcher and carry it to the director of the entertainment." So they carried a pitcher to him. As the director of the entertainment tasted the water that had become wine and did not know from where it came but the attendants who baled up the water knew. The director of entertainment called the bride-groom and said, "Every human being first holds on to the good wine and when they are drunk with intoxication then serves the worst. You have guarded and kept the good wine until now!"

This Yahusha did in *Qanah* (Cana) of *Galiylah* (Galilee) as the commencement of His supernatural indications. This rendered apparent His glory and His pupils had faith and entrusted their spiritual well-being to Him as the Messiah. Yahusha and his pupils stayed with Miryam (Mary) through the winter and then after this He traveled thirty miles north to the town of *Kaphernachuwm* (Capernaum) on the northern shore of the Sea of Galilee and His mother and His brothers and His pupils went with Him and they stayed there a few days.

In early spring of 27 AD Phasaelis, the wife of Tetrarch Herodes Antipater (Herod Antipas) who ruled *Galiylah* (Galilee), found out about the affair he was having with her sister-in-law and about their secret plans of getting married. Therefore, she asked for a divorce and permission to travel to the frontier fortress of Machaerus. Tetrarch Herodes Antipater granted Phasaelis her request and provided military protection until she reached Machaerus safely. As soon as Phasaelis was out of sight a second military escort was dispatched to the palace of his brother Tetrarch Philippos (Herod Phillip) in Northern Syria to get Herodias his wife. Herod Phillip was away on business with Rome which made the little ruse of his wife and brother easy to pull off. When Phasaelis reached the fortress Machaerus Nabatean military forces took over her protection and escorted her to her father King Aretas IV (King of Arabia). With his daughter back safely in his custody, King Aretas IV sent a message to Tetrarch Herodes Antipater that this act of unfaithfulness would lead to open war someday between their borders.

An insulted King Aretas IV of Nabatea (Arabia) and an irate brother Tetrarch Philippos (Herod Phillip) were not the only problems that Tetrarch Herodes Antipater had to deal with. It did not take long until *Yowchanan Matbyl* (John the Baptist) learned of this wife-swapping scheme of Tetrarch Herodes Antipater because

Yowchanan operated on the borders between Nabatea (Arabia) and the territory governed by Tetrarch Herodes Antipater (Herod Antipas). *Yowchanan Matbyl* (John the Baptist) immediately began to publically condemn and speak out against the marriage of Tetrarch Herodes Antipater with his sister-in-law Herodias, who also was his niece. This public shaming did not set well with the Tetrarch but he feared *Yowchanan Matbyl* (John the Baptist) because he viewed him as a prophet of Yahuah. However, Herodes did not fear him or Yahuah and continuously whined about the public embarrassment Yowchanan was causing.

10

Also in the spring of 27 AD, Yahusha, his mother, his brothers and his pupils left *Kaphernachuwm* (Capernaum) and traveled south to Yruwshalaim (Jerusalem) to take part in the annual celebration of *Pecach* (Passover). When Yahusha arrived at the Temple He found in the Temple those selling, bartering and trading as peddler's: oxen, sheep and pigeons along with the money brokers handling coins sitting down at tables. Yahusha quickly made a whip out of ropes and ejected out of the Sacred Temple the sheep, oxen and the coin dealers, pouring forth the coins and overturning the four-legged tables. To those selling and bartering pigeons He commanded, "Take these things from here! Do not make the dwelling of My Father a dwelling of wholesale merchandise." At that time His pupils recollected from the Scriptures that it had been written in *Thillah* 69:9 (Psalm) **"For this reason, the jealousy of Your house has eaten Me."**

Then the Yhudiy (Jews) responded to Him and said, "What supernatural indication do you show to us that you should do such things?" Yahusha responded, "Destroy this Temple and in three days I will construct it." Then the Yhudiy (Jews) remarked, "It took forty-six years to construct this Temple and you will construct it in three days?" However, Yahusha was referring to the Temple of His body. As He was in Yruwshalaim (Jerusalem) at the *Pecach* (Passover), at the festival, many had faith and entrusted their spiritual well-being to the Messiah in the authority and character of His Name and were spectators of His supernatural indications of miracles which He did.

However, Yahusha on His part was not entrusting Himself to the Yhudiy (Jews) because He knew all men and because He did not need anyone to bear witness concerning man for He Himself knew what was in mankind.

While Miryam (Mary) was in the Great City Yruwshalaim (Jerusalem) for the celebration, she went and visited the fan maker Ya'kov Gammed Aer (James Walter Ayers) in the Upper City. Her old neighborhood changed immensely and she could hardly recognize it. The saddest thing was that the old Hasmonaeon Palace of her royal Maccabee heritage was not shielded from public view. The fan maker lived clear to the south end of the Upper City about two blocks from the wall that separated the Upper City from the Lower City. When Ya'kov opened the door to his old family friend Miryam was met with a pleasant surprise. Two weeks ago Ya'kov became the proud father of a new baby boy named Yirmyah Achuw Aer (Jerry Lee Ayers). Little Yirmyah ben Ya'kov had a name with a meaning of 'Yahuah will raise a meadow with breath'. They caught up on old times and Miryam told them about Yahusha being the Anointed Messiah, a secret she had kept silent for thirty years. At first the news was hard to believe but in the end they wanted to go hear Him teach.

While in Yruwshalaim Yahusha met a very powerful ruler among the Yhudiy (Jews) named Nikodemos. He was a member of the Parash (Pharisee Sect) and possessed political clout among the other *kohens* (priests). Nikodemos came to Yahusha at night and said to him, "Rhabbi, we know that You have come as a teacher from Yahuah because not even one is able to do these supernatural indications of miracles which You do unless Yahuah is with You." Yahusha responded to him, "Firmly and surely, I relate in words to you, unless one is regenerated from above, he is not able to see the royalty, realm and rule of Yahuah." Nikodemos expressed to

Him, "How is a human being able to be procreated of a father and a mother being aged? He is not able to enter into the matrix cavity of his mother a second time and be procreated?" Yahusha explained, "Firmly and surely I relate in words to you, unless one is regenerated of water and Sacred Breath (Holy Spirit) he is not able to enter into the royalty, realm and rule of Yahuah! That procreated by a father and mother from the flesh is flesh. That regenerated from the Sacred Breath is breath like a spirit. Do not be in admiration because I said to you, it is necessary for you to be regenerated anew from above. The Sacred Breath breathes hard like a breeze where He chooses and His voice you hear, but you do not know from where He comes and where He withdraws as if sinking out of sight. In this way is everyone having been regenerated from the Sacred Breath (Holy Spirit)."

Nikodemos responded and said to Him, "How can these things come into being?" Yahusha looked into his eyes and answered, "You are the teacher of Yisra'Yah (Israel) and you do not know these things? Firmly and surely I relate to you in words as a set discourse, We know what We talk about and what We have stared at to be a witness and testify and Our evidence given, you refused to receive and get a hold of it. If I told you about worldly things and you did not respect them then if I speak to you about the things above the sky, how will you have faith and entrust your spiritual well-being to the Messiah? Not even one has gone up into Heaven, the eternal abode of Yahuah except He who descended down out of Heaven, who is the Son of Man. As Mosheh (Moses) elevated the cunning snake in the lonesome wasteland, in this way it is necessary for the Son of Man to be elevated in order that everyone having faith and entrusting their spiritual well-being to the Anointed Messiah, in Him, may not perish but possess perpetual life. For this reason, in this way Yahuah loved the world, therefore He gave His only born

Son in order that everyone who has faith and entrusts their spiritual well- being to the Anointed Messiah, in Him, will not perish but possess perpetual life."

Yahusha continued, "For this reason, Yahuah did not send the Son on a mission into the world that He condemn the world but that the world may be saved and protected through Him. The ones having faith and entrusting their spiritual well-being to the Anointed Messiah are not condemned and punished. But the ones not having faith and entrusting their spiritual well-being to the Anointed Messiah has even now been condemned because they have not had faith and entrusted their spiritual well-being into the authority and character of the name of the only born Son of Yahuah. This is the justice of divine law that the shining rays of light have come into the world and human beings loved the obscure shadiness more than the shining rays of light. For this reason, their actions and work were hurtful, malicious, vicious and evil. For this reason, everyone practicing repeatedly and habitually wickedness hates the shining rays of light and does not come to the shining rays of light, in order that his work and actions may not be admonished. But the one doing the truth comes to the shining rays of light in order that his works and actions may be rendered apparent because they are being engaged to toil in Yahuah."

After this Yahusha took His four pupils and left Yruwshalaim (Jerusalem) and stayed eight months in northeast Yhuwdah (Judea) as his pupils learned to baptize by submerging to make fully wet. *Yowchanan Matbyl* (John the Baptist) also moved north to Samaria to preach and baptize. He stationed himself for baptism in Ayin meaning 'fountain' near Saleim because there were many waters from rain. Crowds approached near and appeared publicly to be submerged to make fully wet in baptism. That is why *Yowchanan Matbyl* (John the

Baptist) was not thrown into the guarded place by Tetrarch Herodes Antipater (Herod Antipas). Accordingly, the pupils of Yowchanan were disputing with leaders of Yhuwdah (Judea) with respect to washing off. They came to *Yowchanan Matbyl* (John the Baptist) and complained to him, "Rhabbi, the One who was with you across the Yarden River (Jordan River) to whom you have testified as a witness to, you see He submerged to make fully wet in baptism and all are coming to Him."

Yowchanan Matbyl (John the Baptist) responded to them, "A human being is not able to take and get a hold of anything unless it has been given to him from Heaven, the eternal abode of Yahuah. You, yourselves are a witness to me that I testified and said, I am not the Messiah but that I have been sent on a mission in front of the Messiah. He possessing the veiled bride is the bride-groom, but the friend of the bride-groom standing and hears him is happy and cheerful with delight for the voice of the bride-groom. Accordingly, this cheerfulness of delight has verified the prediction of me. It is necessary for that One to enlarge but I to be less of an influence. The One that has been first from above coming is above rank of all. The one being of the soil of the globe is of the soil of the globe and of the soil of the globe he talks. He coming from Heaven, the eternal abode of Yahuah is above in rank over all. What He has stared at and heard, this He is a witness and testifies and His testimony not even one takes and gets a hold of. He receiving and taking a hold of His testimony has stamped for security that Yahuah is true. For this reason, whom Yahuah sends on a mission talks the utterances of Yahuah and He gives the Sacred Breath (Holy Spirit) without a limited portion. The Father loves the Son and all things have been given into His hand of power. The one having faith and entrusting one's spiritual well-being to the Anointed Messiah, to the Son has perpetual life. But the one willfully and perversely disbelieving the Son will not see life but punishment of Yahuah will remain upon him." Not long after this discourse Tetrarch Herodes Antipater (Herod Antipas) had *Yowchanan Matbyl* (John the Baptist) imprisoned down in the dungeon inside the guarded place of the military outpost of Machaerus.

During the late spring on the day of *Chag HaChamishshiym* (Feast of the Fifty) which was also called in the Greek language Pentecost, Yahusha left the territory of northeastern Yhuwdah (Judea) and headed towards his territory of nativity *Galiylah* (Galilee). He had to travel through Samaria first but the rumor of His fame issued out through all the region around *Galiylah* (Galilee) in regards to Him. Accordingly, Yahusha knew that the Parash (Pharisee Sect) had complained to *Yowchanan Matbyl* (John the Baptist) that He had submerged to make fully wet in baptism more pupils than Yowchanan. Therefore, Yahusha Himself did not do the submerging to make fully wet in baptism but instead His pupils did.

As the band of Yahusha was traveling through Shomrown (Samaria) on their way to *Galiylah* (Galilee) they came into a town of Shomrown (Samaria) called Shekar meaning 'intensely alcoholic liquor' near the plot of ground that Yisra'Yah (Israel/Jacob) had given to his son Yowceph (Joseph). There was a plump gushing water fountain of Yisra'Yah (Israel) at that location. Yahusha was feeling fatigued from the travel so He sat down by the gushing fountain and it was about the sixth hour (noon). A woman of Shomrown (Samaria) came to dip with her bucket to bale up the water. Yahusha related in words to her, "Give Me a drink!" His pupils had departed into the town in order that they could purchase in the market rations for nourishment. The Shomrown'iy (Samaritan) woman expressed with concern to Him, "How do You being a Yhudiy (Jew) ask from me to drink, since I am a Shomrown'iy (Samaritan) woman? Yhudiy

(Jews) do not associate with Shomrown'iy (Samaritians)!" Yahusha responded, "If you knew the Gratuity of Yahuah and Who is the One relating in words to you, give Me a drink you would have Him and He would have given you Living Water!"

The woman expressed to Him, "Master, you do not possess a baling vessel and the hole for the well is deep. Accordingly, from where do You possess Living Water? You are not greater than our father, Yisra'Yah (Israel/Jacob) who gave us this well and he drank out of it and his sons and his stock raised on the farm?" Yahusha answered her, "Everyone drinking of this water will thirst once more. But whoever drinks of the water which I will give to him in no way will thirst until the Messianic period. The water which I give to him will become in Him a plump gushing fountain of water gushing and jumping to perpetual life." The woman begged, "Master give me this water that I not thirst or come here to this spot to dip my bucket to bale up water!" Yahusha addressed her and said, "Withdraw and address your husband by name and come here." The woman bowed her head in shame and said, "I do not possess a husband." Yahusha related in a set discourse, "You spoke well I do not possess a husband. For this reason, you possessed five husbands and now whom you possess is not your husband! This thing you have uttered in truth."

The woman bowed to the ground and said, "Master, I discern that You are an inspired prophet. Our fathers prostrated themselves in homage for reverence and adoration on this mountain but You say that in Yruwshalaim is the necessary location where to prostrate ourselves in homage for reverence and adoration." Yahusha bent down and lightly touched her shoulder and with reassurance said, "Woman have faith and entrust your spiritual well-being to the Messiah, Me, that an hour will come when neither on this mountain or in the city of Yruwshalaim you will prostrate yourself in homage for reverence and adoration to the Father. You prostrate yourself in homage for reverence and adoration to what you do not know but we prostrate ourselves in homage for reverence and adoration to what we know because *Yahusha* (salvation) being rescued for safety is from the Yhudiy (Jews). However an hour is coming and is now, when the truthful worshipers will prostrate themselves in homage for reverence and adoration to the Father in the breath of the spirit and truth. For this reason, the Father seeks this sort of those prostrating themselves in homage for reverence and adoration to Him. Yahuah is Breath of Spirit and those prostrating themselves in homage for reverence and adoration to Him are necessary to prostrate themselves in the Breath of Spirit and truth." The woman said to Him, "I know that the Messiah is coming, the One called the Anointed Messiah when that One comes, He will announce in detail to us all things." Yahusha then replied, "I Exist, He that is talking to you." Just then, His pupils came and were astonished that He was talking with the woman. However, not even one asked, "What are you seeking? Why do you speak to her?"

Then the woman left her water jar at the well and departed into the town to tell the story of what happened to the rest of the town folk. She exclaimed, "Come! See a Man who spoke to me all things whatever I did. Is this One not the Messiah?" Then the whole town came out to Him. Now in the meantime his pupils requested Him expressing in words, "Master, eat!" But He said to them, "I possess food to eat which you do not know." So, the pupils said to one another, whether any brought Him something to eat." Yahusha overheard their conversations and knowing their thoughts said, "My food is in order that I may do the purpose of Him that dispatched Me and I may accomplish and compete His work. Do you not say it is four months yet and the reaping of the crop comes? Look now!

I relate to you in words, raise up your eyes and look at the territory because even now the fields are white to reap the crop. He harvesting the crop takes and gets a hold of the pay for services and collects plucked fruit to perpetual life that also he scattering to sow at the same place and time may be cheerful and happy with him harvesting the crop. In this the Anointed Messiah is true, that a different one scatters to sow and a different one harvests the crop. I sent you out on a mission to harvest the crop what you have not worked hard and felt fatigued over. Different ones have worked hard and felt fatigued and you have entered into their pain of toil."

From out of that town of the Shomrown'iy (Samaritans) many had faith and entrusted their spiritual well-being to the Messiah, in Him because of what the woman had said, testifying as a witness that, 'He spoke to me all things whatever I had done.' Accordingly, in that manner, the Shomrown'iy (Samaritans) came to Him and they requested Him to stay with them. So He, along with His four pupils stayed there for two days. Therefore, many more had faith and entrusted their spiritual well-being to the Messiah through what He said. Then they said to the woman, "No longer because of your talk do we have faith in Him, the Messiah, because we ourselves have heard and we know that this One is truly the Deliverer, the Messiah of the world."

After the two days, He issued out from there into *Galiylah* (Galilee) in the summer of 27 AD. Yahusha warned His pupils and testified Himself that an inspired prophet in his own native town of his fatherland does not possess value or dignity. When Yahusha entered into the territory of *Galiylah* (Galilee), He heralded like a public crier the good message of the Gospel of Yahuah saying, "The set and proper time of the predictions has been finished and verified. Now the royalty, realm and rule of Yahuah approaches near! Think differently, reconsider and feel moral compunction and have faith to entrust your spiritual well-being to the Messiah, heralding the good message of the gospel!" He taught in their synagogues of assembled persons and was being rendered glorious by all who heard Him. Thus the people in the territory of *Galiylah* (Galilee) openly received Him since some of them had seen all the things which He had done in Yruwshalaim (Jerusalem) at the festival.

11

While Yahusha was in *Galiylah* (Galilee) during the summer of 27 AD, He came once more to Qanah (Cana) where He made the water into wine. While there He met a sovereign whose son was very sick and feeble with disease in the town of Kaphernachuwm (Capernaum). He had heard that Yahusha had come from Yhuwdah (Judea) into the territory of *Galiylah* (Galilee) and the sovereign had departed from his city to seek out Yahusha. The sovereign requested that Yahusha would come to Kaphernachuwm (Capernaum) and cure his son because he was about to die. Yahusha said to him, "Unless you see supernatural indications of miracles and omens you refuse to have faith and entrust your spiritual well-being to the Messiah." The sovereign pleaded with Him, "Master, please come with me prior to my child dying." Yahusha having compassion said to him, "Travel because your son lives!" At that moment, the sovereign had faith and entrusted his spiritual well-being to the Messiah in what Yahusha the Messiah had said to him and he traveled back home.

As the sovereign traveled back to the city of Kaphernachuwm (Capernaum) his slaves encountered him and announced relating in words, "Your child lives!" Accordingly, he asked from them the hour in which he began to get well and they said to him, "Yesterday, at the seventh hour (1:00 pm) the inflamed fever left him." The father knew that in that hour it was when Yahusha had said to him, "Your son lives!" When the sovereign returned home, he himself, and his whole family had faith and entrusted their spiritual well-being to the Messiah. Once more this was the second supernatural indication miracle Yahusha having come from Yhuwdah (Judea) into *Galiylah* (Galilee) had done.

During that summer when He left Qanah (Cana) Yahusha traveled back south ten miles to His home town of Nazareth. As He approached Nazareth He became wound up tight like a toy and He went in as was His habit, on the *Shabbath* (Sabbath) into the synagogue of assembled persons and stood up to read the Scriptures like He used to. A roll of Ysha'ah (Isaiah) the inspired prophet was given over to Him and He found the location where it was written in chapter sixty-one verses one and two, **"The Sacred Breath of Master Yahuah is on Me. For Yahuah has anointed Me to announce the Good News to the depressed. He has sent Me out to wrap firmly with a turban to stop the dejected heart and to call out loud freedom to the captives and to those yoked and hitched. I will open the dungeon and deliver them salvation** (Yahusha) **from the jail of sin and to call out loud the year of cheerfulness of Yahuah and the day of vengeance of Yahuah and to console all those lamenting."** Closing the roll He gave it back to the assistant and He sat down. All of the eyes in the synagogue of assembled personas were gazing intently at Him. Then He said to them, "Today has verified the prediction of this Holy Writ of Scriptures in your ears!"

The assemblage of persons in the synagogue were all testifying to Him and admired at what was said with such graciousness that discharged from His mouth. They said, "Is this not Yahusha ben Yowceph (Yahshua son of Joseph)?" Yahusha responded, "Entirely you will speak this parable of common life conveying a moral truth to Me, 'Physician heal Yourself! What things we heard come into being in Kaphernachuwm (Capernaum), do also in this spot, in Your native town of Your father's land. Firmly, I relate to you in words as a set discourse, that no inspired prophet is approved in his native town of his fatherland. But on a truth I relate in words to you, many widows were in the days of Eliyah (Elijah) in Yisra'Yah (Israel) when the sky was closed for over three years and six months, when a great destitution because of scarcity of food was upon all that region of soil. Not even one of them Eliyah (Elijah) was sent to except to Tsarphath of Tsiydown to a woman, a widow. There were many scaly lepers during the time of Eliysha (Elisha) the inspired prophet and not even one of them was cleansed in Yisra'Yah (Israel) except Na'aman the Tsor'iy (Syrian)." All in the synagogue of the assemblage of persons heard these things and were filled with passion and began breathing hard in furious anger. They stood up and ejected Him outside the town and led Him up to the brink of a cliff of the hill on which their town was constructed in order to throw him down. However, He traveled through the middle of them and moved on."

In the Autumn Yahusha having abandoned and left behind Nazareth, He came and permanently resided in a house in Kaphernachuwm (Capernaum) along the Sea of *Galiylah* (Galilee), in the regions of Zbuwluwn and Naphtaliy in order to verify the prediction of what was spoken through the inspired prophet Ysha'Yah (Isaiah) chapter nine verses one and two, **"Region of Zbuwluwn and region of Naphtaliy, the route of the sea across the Yardan River, Galiylah** (Galilee) **The people who sat down to remain in the obscurity of shadiness saw a big shining ray and to those who have sat down to remain in the territory and the dark shadow of death manifested light rays rose up to them."** From that time Yahusha commenced to herald as a public crier the gospel and laying forth words pleaded, "Think differently and prick your conscience! For this reason the royalty, realm and rule of the heavens, the eternal abode of Yahweh has approached and come near." The people were struck with astonishment at His teaching because He was teaching them as possessing privilege and delegated influence with force and not in the same manner as the scribes.

As Yahusha tread all around and walked at large near the fishing village of *Beth-tsaida* (Bethsaida) by the harp-shaped Lake Kinnrowth also known as the Sea of *Galiylah* (Galilee) He saw two sailing vessels standing near the shore of the lake. However the fishing sailors had disembarked from them and were rinsing off the fishing seines. He saw the two brothers Shim'own (Simon), the one called Petros in the Greek language, meaning a piece of rock and his brother Andreas (Andrew) who were throwing a small round fishing net into the sea because they were fishers of salt water. After walking aboard their sailing vessel Yahusha requested Shim'own to put out to sea from the shore somewhat of a puny distance. There Yahusha sat down and taught the small throng of rabble from the sailing vessel who had gathered at the seashore. After He stopped talking, He spoke to Shim'own (Simon Peter) and said, "Put out and return to the mystery of the sea and cast by lowering your fishing seines into the void for a haul of caught fish." Shim'own responded and said to Him, "Teacher we have worked hard, even feeling fatigued throughout all the night and we took nothing, but at Your command I will lower the fishing seines into the void of the sea." Doing this thing Shim'own and Andreas shut together the seines containing a large populace of fish and their fishing seines were beginning to tear asunder.

At once, they signaled their partners those in the other sailing vessel to come and give them aide. They came and filled both of the sailing vessels and they began to sink. Having seen this Shim'own Kepha (Simon Peter) prostrated himself in homage towards the knees of Yahusha and trembling said, "Issue forth from me because I exist as a sinful man, Master!" Shim'own was dumbfounded and clasped with astonishment along with all the ones with Him at the haul of the fish they captured. Yahusha said to them, "Do not be alarmed, from now on you will be capturing and ensnaring to take alive human beings. Come and follow behind My back and I will make you fishers of human beings!" They at once put away the fishing seines and became united with Him on the same road as disciples. After they got out of the boat and walked forward down the shore a puny distance from there, Yahusha saw two different brothers the partners of Shim'own and Andreas, Ya'kov ben Zabdiy (James son of Zebedee) and Yowchanan (John) his brother, both first cousins of Yahusha since their mother Shalowmit (Salome) and Miryam (Mary) were sisters. They were in the sailing vessel with Zabdiy (Zebedee) their father repairing thoroughly their fishing seine from the large haul, and He called them. They at once moored the sailing vessels onto the shore and went forth from the vessels and their father with the workers for a wage and became united on the same road with Him.

Then they entered into the synagogue of Kaphernachuwm (Capernaum) on the Shabbath. In their synagogue of assemblage of persons was a human being possessing a lewd and wicked demonic spirit and he screamed out loud with a bestial tone of voice screeching, "Aha! What do You want with us, Yahusha of Nazareth? Did You come to destroy us fully? I know You, who You are, the sacred and blameless One of Yahuah!" Then Yahusha admonished and forbade him saying, "Be muzzled and issue forth from out of him!" Then the demonic spirit hurled and flung him with a quick toss in the middle and threw him into a spasmodic contraction and mangled him convulsing with epilepsy. As it croaked like a screaming raven it shrieked with a loud tone and he came out of him. All those present in the synagogue were surprised and astounded so much that they discussed among themselves saying, "What is this new and fresh instruction that with privilege and delegated influence even the demonic spirits He gave orders and they conform to the authority of His command?" The things heard about His actions at once issued out of the synagogue like a roar of a rumor and into all the region of *Galiylah* (Galilee).

As soon as they issued out of the synagogue of assemblage of persons, Yahusha came into the residence of Shim'own Kepha (Simon Peter) and Andreas (Andrew) with Yak'ov (James) and Yowchanan (John). He saw the mother of Shim'own's wife having been thrown down sick and set on fire with a fever. So He touched her hands and the inflammation of fever was sent away at once. Then she collected her faculties and became aroused from lying down with a disease and she waited upon them as a host. When late afternoon the eve of night fall had come and the sun sank down deep in the west, they rendered to Him many exercised by demons. There were so many it was if the whole town was collected at the house by the door. So He laid his hands on each one of them and relieved them of their diseases. He ejected the evil spirits by speaking His thoughts but He would not allow the demons to speak because they knew Him to be the Anointed Messiah. However, they did shriek and screamed loud like croaking ravens in the spiritual realm, "You are the Anointed Messiah, the Son of Yahuah." Also, all those who were morally and physically bad were waited upon menially and relieved of their diseases by Him in order that what was spoken through the inspired prophet Ysha'Yah (Isaiah) may be verified and finished what was predicted, **"He took and held our frailties and feebleness of mind and body and He removed our maladies."**

Very early in the night, He stood up and issued out and went to a location in the lonesome wasteland and was in that place praying in worship to Yahuah. Then Shim'own (Simon) and those with him searched for and hunted Him down. When they found Him they said, "All are seeking You." He responded, "Let us pass into the remote cities without walls in order that to herald as a public crier the divine truth of the Gospel likewise in those places because this is the purpose that I issued forth." When it became daytime, He traveled from the lonesome wasteland and the throng of rabble that had sought Him out, came up to Him and held Him tightly so He did not travel from them. Instead He spoke to them, "It is necessary for Me to also announce the good news and evangelize the Gospel of the royalty, realm and rule of Yahuah to other towns because I was sent out on this mission" Therefore, Yahusha walked all around *Galiylah* (Galilee) teaching in their meeting places of an assemblage of persons, the synagogues and heralded as a public crier the divine truth and the good message of the gospel of the royalty realm and rule. He also waited upon menially to relive diseases, every malady and debility among the people. The hearing of His actions departed into all Tsor (Syria). They began to bear towards Him all those possessing physical or moral badness, various maladies and disabilities and those compressing their ears because of torture and those exercised by demons, and crazy ones that howled at the moon and paralytics. Yahusha waited upon all of them menially and relieved them of their diseases. Large throngs of rabble became united on the same road as Him from *Galiylah* and *Dekopolis*, the ten city region and Yruwshalaim and Yhuwdah and across the Yarden (Jordan) River.

One day it happened when He existed in one of the towns, a man completely covered with scaly leprosy came to Him and falling on his knees and the front of his face and he begged as he bound himself to the petition saying, "If You wish, You are able to cleanse me!" Then Yahusha felt sympathy and His bowels yearned with pity and stretched by extending His hand. Then He touched him and said, "I wish too, be cleansed!" As soon as He had said this the scaly leprosy departed from him and he was cleansed. Before He sent him away Yahusha instructed, "Look here, do not speak by word or writing to not even one anything but withdraw and show yourself to the *kohen* (priest) and tender with respect to your washing off, what Mosheh (Moses) enjoined as evidence given to the priesthood." However, the former leper issued out and commenced to herald as a public crier much about the divine truth of the Gospel. This topic was divulged and reported thoroughly in order that He was not able any further to enter publically in plain sight into a town. Instead, he was outside in lonesome wasteland locations but the people came to Him from all directions.

In the early winter of 28 AD He entered once more into the city of Kaphernachuwm (Capernaum) and through a period of days it was heard that He was in a dwelling there. At once many were collected together, therefore no further was there any space not even to the door and He spoke to them the topic. As He was teaching some of the *Parash* (Pharisee Sect) and the teachers of the Jewish Law were sitting down, who had come from out of every hamlet of *Galiylah* (Galilee) and Yhuwdah (Judea) and Yruwshalaim (Jerusalem). The miraculous power of Yahuah was present for the purpose of Him to cure. They came carrying to Him a paralytic on a couch of sickness being lifted and taken up by four men. Not being able to approach near to Him through the throng of rabble they unroofed the clay tiles and the thatched roof whichever spot He was. After digging out and removing the roof they lowered the mattress on which the paralytic was lying down on. Yahusha saw their moral conviction of religious truth especially to rely upon the Messiah for salvation and He related in words to the paralytic, "Child to you is sent away your sins."

Some of the scribes were sitting there and reckoned thoroughly and deliberated in their hearts, "Why does this One in this way, utter words of vilification against Yahuah? Which is able to send away sins except One, Yahuah?" At once Yahusha knew in His Sacred Breath that in this way through their internal consideration and external debate that they reckoned thoroughly and deliberated among themselves. So he spoke to them "Why do you reckon thoroughly and deliberate these things in your hearts? What is better for toil to say to the paralytic your sins are sent away or to say arouse from your disease and lift up your mattress and walk at large! But in order that you may know by sight that the Son of Man has the privilege and delegated influence upon the soil of the globe to send away sins." Then He related in words to the paralytic, "I relate to you words in a set discourse, rouse up from your disease and lift up your mattress and withdraw to your dwelling. At once, he aroused from lying with disease. Then lifting up the mattress he issued out in front of all, thus therefore all were put out of their wits and astounded and rendered glorious to Yahuah relating in words "We have never seen anything in this way."

Yahusha issued out once more beside the sea and all the throng of rabble came to Him and he taught them. Then He went away and saw *Leviy Mattithiyah* (Levi Matthew) the son of Cheleph sitting down at the tax gatherer's place of business and He related to him in words, "Come and be united with Me and accompany Me as a disciple!" Mattithiyah (Matthew) stood up, abandoned and left behind all things and became united on the road in the same way with and accompanied Him as a disciple. That evening Mattithiyah made a great reception with convivial entertainment with humor and laughter for Yahusha at his residence. It came into being while He was in the residence of Mattithiyah (Matthew) many tax farmers who collected public revenue and sinners reclined in the company with Yahusha and His pupils at a meal because they were many and they became united with Yahusha to accompany Him as pupils. The scribes and members of the *Parash* (Pharisee Sect) saw Him eating with tax farmers who collect public revenue and sinners and grumbled to His pupils, "Why does He eat and drink with the tax farmers who collect public revenue and sinners?" Yahusha heard this and rebutted them, "Those who can exercise force and have sound health possess not an occasion or requirement of a physician but those possessing physical badness. Teachers of the Jewish Law learn what this means. 'I prefer human compassion and not the actions or victims of sacrifice.' You see, I did not come to call the innocent of character or holy in actions but sinners to have compunction of guilt and to reverse their decisions."

After these things it was now the spring of 28 AD and it was time of the festival of the Yhudiy (Jews) called *Pecach* (Passover). Yahusha went down to Yruwshalaim (Jerusalem) to celebrate His second *Pecach* (Passover) since He began His ministry. In Yruwshalaim is the Sheep Gate and near the gate is a pond for bathing and swimming which in Hebraisti (Aramaic) is called, Beyth-Checed meaning 'House of Kindness'. It possessed five rectangular squares surrounded by colonnades. In these was a large throng of rabble of the feeble, the blind, the limping and the withered ones lying down sick. There was a certain human being who had been feeble for thirty-eight years. Yahusha saw this one lying down sick and knowing that he had been in that condition even now much time, related to him in words, "Do you wish to become healthy!" The feeble one responded to Him, "Master, I do not possess a human being that when the water is stirred and agitated to rolling water that he will throw me into the bathing pond! But as I am coming, a different one descends down in front of me." Yahusha answered him, "Rise up, lift and take up your mattress and walk and tread all around!" At once the human being became healthy and lifted and took up his mattress and walked and treaded all around.

On that day it was a Shabbath (day of rest). Accordingly, the Yhudiy (Jews) said to the one having been relieved of the disease, "It is a Shabbath. It is not right being out in public for you to lift the mattress!" He responded to them, "The One making me healthy, that One said to me lift and take up your mattress and walk and tread all around." Accordingly, they interrogated him saying, "Who is the Man who spoke to you, lift and take up your mattress and walk and tread all around?" But he that was cured did not know who it was because Yahusha had slipped off into the throng of rabble being in that location. After these things Yahusha found him in the temple and said to him, "You have become healthy. Sin no further lest a more evil and aggravated thing comes into being to you!" The human being departed and announced in detail to the Yhuwdiy (Jews) that Yahusha was He that made him healthy. Because of this thing the Yhuwdiy (Jews) pursued to persecute Yahusha and sought to kill Him outright for the things He did on the Shabbath (day of rest).

Yahusha announced to the Yhuwdiy (Jews), "My Father toils this very day, so I toil." The Yhuwdiy (Jews) because of this thing sought even more to kill Him outright because He not only loosened the Shabbath (day of rest) but also expressed that His Father was Yahuah making Himself similar to Yahuah. Yahusha responded and said to them, "Firmly and surely I relate to you in words as a set discourse, the Son is not able to do from Himself anything unless He looks at what the Father is doing. For this reason whatever that One does these things also the Son does similarly. The Father loves the Son and shows to Him all things which He does. Also, greater actions of work than these He will show Him that you may be filled with admiration. Exactly like the Father roused up the dead and revitalizes to life so also the Son who He chooses, He will revitalize to life. The Father does not judicially condemn anyone but the justice of divine law He has given to the Son in order that all may revere the Son just as they revere the Father. He who does not value in the highest degree the Son does not value or revere the Father, the One who dispatched Him. I tell you the one hearing the Messiah, Me, and has faith and entrusts one's spiritual well-being to the Messiah from the One who dispatched Me, has perpetual life and does not come into the Divine Law of justice but has changed places from out of death into life."

As the Yhuwdiy (Jews) grumbled Yahusha continued teaching, "Firmly and surely I relate to you in words as a set discourse an hour comes and now is when the dead corpses will hear the tone of the voice of the Son of Yah (abbreviated Yahuah) and those hearing will live. Exactly like the Father has life in Himself so He gave to the Son to possess life in Himself. He gave the privilege of delegated influence to Him also to do justice by Divine Law because He is the Son of Man. Do not be filled in admiration at this, because an hour comes in which all those in the places of burial will hear the tone of His voice and will proceed out. Those that have done good into the standing up again for a resurrection from death into life but those having practiced wickedness into a standing up again for a resurrection from death into the justice of Divine Law. I am not able to do from Myself anything. Just as I hear, I condemn and punish. My justice of Divine Law is innocent in character and holy in actions because I do not seek My purpose but the purpose of the Father dispatching Me. If I am a witness and testify with respect to Myself then My judicial evidence given is not true. There is a different One who is a witness and testifies with respect to Me and I know that the judicial evidence given is true which He is a witness and testifies with respect to Me. You have sent out on a mission to *Yowchanan Matbyl* (John the Baptist) and he has been a witness and testified to the truth."

"I did not take and get a hold of the judicial evidence given by a human being but these things I say to you, in order that you may be delivered through salvation *(Yahusha)* for protection. That one was the portable lamp set on fire and shining light. You were willing to jump for joy for an hour in his shining rays of light. But I possess the judicial evidence given greater than *Yowchanan Matbyl* (John the Baptist). For this reason, the toil and actions which has been given to Me from the Father that I may accomplish them to completion. The toil and actions that I do themselves are a witness and testify with respect to Me, that the Father has sent Me out on a mission. He, the Father, dispatched Me and He has been a witness and testifies with regard to Me. Not even the tone of His voice have you heard at any time or have you seen His form. His Messiah you do not possess to stay in you because He sent that one, *Yowchanan Matbyl* (John the Baptist), and you do not have faith to entrust your spiritual well-being to the Messiah being this One. You investigate the Scriptures of Holy Writ because you think in them you possess perpetual life and those are the ones being a witness and testify with respect to me. You do not choose to come to Me in order that you may possess life."

He continued speaking to the scribes, "I do not take to get a hold of glory from human beings but I have known you that the love of Yahuah you do not possess in yourselves! I have come in the authority and character of the Name of My Father any of you did not take to get a hold of what I have offered. If a different one comes in the authority and character of their own name, that one you will take and get a hold of what they offer. How can you have faith and entrust your spiritual well-being in the Messiah when you take and get a hold of the glory from one another but do not seek the glory from the only Yahuah? Do you not think that I will charge you with some offence as a plaintiff to the Father? There is already one being a plaintiff and charging you with offences, Mosheh (Moses) in whom you have placed your confidence. For this reason if you had faith and entrusted your spiritual well-being to the Messiah through Mosheh (Moses) then you would have had faith and entrusted your spiritual well-being to the Messiah, in Me. For this reason Mosheh wrote with respect to Me. For if the writing of Mosheh you did have faith in the Messiah, how will you have faith to entrust your spiritual well-being to the Messiah by My utterances?"

Then the pupils of *Yowchanan Matbyl* (John the Baptist) approached and questioned Yahusha, "Why do we and the Parash (Pharisee Sect) abstain from food religiously much but Your pupils do not abstain from food for religious reasons?" Yahusha answered them, "The kinship of the bridal groom are not able to grieve as long as the bridegroom is amidst their company. But the days will come when the bridegroom will be removed from them and then they will abstain from food for religious purposes." Then He related in words as a parable of common life conveying a moral truth to them teaching, "No one stitches upon by fastening with a needle a patch from a new piece of cloth on an antique and worn out dress but its fullness lifts up raises away from the dress and a more aggravated split or gap comes into being. They also do not throw new fermented and fresh intoxicating wine into antique and worn out leathern skin bags used as bottles. As a result the new wine will crack the leathern skin bags used as bottles and they will shatter into minute fragments and the wine pours forth and the leathern skin bags used as bottles are fully destroyed. Instead they throw new and fresh wine into new and fresh leathern skin bags used as bottles and both are conserved from ruin. No one drinking antique wine wishes for new and fresh wine but instead the antique is more useful."

Following this debate and teaching, Yahusha and His disciples left the Great City of Yruwshalaim (Jerusalem) and returned towards the territory of *Galiylah* (Galilee). His followers increased into a large caravan making the scribes and Pharisees jealous because their followers had diminished. Now the *Parash* (Pharisee Sect) would watch carefully every move and scrutinize every syllable that proceeded from His mouth. The power of His teaching and wisdom could not be denied by the religious elite yet the shining rays of light of the truth of the Good News of the Gospel became bitterness in their ritualistic souls giving hope of victory to the dark lord Satan who was plotting with all his evil imagination and scheming thoughts. Ironically those who should have been embracing the light were trying to put it out in order to stay in the darkness of their lost souls.

12

Later on in the spring of 28 AD as Yahusha traveled through the territory of *Galiylah* (Galilee) it became the Shabbath and His little group traveled through the sown planted fields. His pupils were very famished and commenced to pull off heads of grain from the standing stalks to make a road. They took the heads of grain and rubbed out the kernels from the heads of grain with their hands and ate them. When the Parash (Pharisee Sect) saw this they questioned Him, "See here! Your pupils are doing what is not right to do in public on the Shabbath!" Yahusha answered them, "Have you not ever read what David did when he was famished himself and those with him? How he entered into the dwelling of Yahuah at the time that Ebyathar was *Gadowl Kohen* (High Priest) and ate the raised loaves of bread the show-bread exposed to Yahuah which was not right for him to do in public and neither those with him except merely for priests? Or have you not read in the Law of Mosheh (Moses) that on the Shabbaths the priests in the sacred place desecrate the Shabbath and are innocent? I relate to you in words that One greater than the sacred place is here. But if you had known what it is when it was said, '***I prefer and choose divine active compassion and not sacrifice you would not have pronounced guilty the innocent***'. Do you not know that the Shabbath came into being because of human beings and not human beings for the Shabbath? For this reason the Son of Man is also Master of the Shabbath."

On the next Shabbath, Yahusha and His pupils went to the

synagogue to teach and there was a man possessing a hand like the shrunken earth from the scorching sun and the Parash (Pharisee Sect) inquired of Him, "Is it right to do in public to relive diseases on the Shabbath?" They were insidiously and scrupulously inspecting Him to see if He would heal on the Shabbath so they could find a complaint or charge Him with a criminal offence. He knew their internal considerations and external debates so Yahusha smiled though His beard and answered, "I will ask you one thing. What will be of you if a human being would possess one sheep and if this one sheep falls into a cistern hole in the ground on the Shabbath. Would he not use all his strength to seize it and raise it up from ruin and disease? Certainly does not a human being surpass a sheep? Is it also right being out in public on the Shabbath to be a well-doer as a favor or duty or to be a bad-doer to injure or sin or to save and protect the vitality of breath or kill outright?" The Parash (Pharisee Sect) was hushed and did not speak. Yahusha looked all around at them with violent passion of justifiable anger being afflicted with sorrow because of the stupidity and callousness of their hard hearts. Suddenly He broke the silence and said, "This therefore it is right to do morally well in public on the Shabbath." Then He said to the man with the withered hand, "Rise up in the middle of this assemblage and extend your hand!" So the man extended it and it was reconstituted healthy in the same manner as the other hand. However, at once the Parash (Pharisee Sect) were filled with stupidity and rage and stomped out and hustled to the Herodianoi (Herodians-members of the Herod family and political party.) making a lay court for advisement from a deliberative body against Him and they considered in what manner they could fully destroy Him so that He would perish.

Therefore that evening, Yahusha knew about it and retired from there to the sea. While He was by the sea many throngs of rabble joined Him as disciples. They came from the territory of *Galiylah* (Galilee), Yhuwdah (Judea), the Great City of Yruwshalaim (Jerusalem), Edom, the cities of Tsor (Tyre) and Tsiydown (Sidon) and even from across the Yarden River (Jordan River). The large crowd of rabble pressed hard upon Him so He asked His pupils that a boat should be brought close to Him in order that the crowd would not press upon Him. He relieved all of them of their diseases and they embraced Him in order that they could touch Him. When the demonic spirits became spectators of Him they fell towards Him in homage and croaked like screaming ravens shrieking and moaning, "You are the Son of Yahuah!" He forbade and admonished them that they should not make Him apparent publically so that what was uttered by the inspired prophet Ysha'Yah (Isaiah) in chapter forty-two would evidence to finish the prediction stating, "**Look here! My Boy beaten with impunity in whom I made a choice My Beloved in whom My vitality of Sacred Breath has thought well of and approved. I will place My Sacred Breath on Him and He will announce justice from the judicial bench of Divine Law to foreign races and tribes. He will not even wrangle or clamor. Neither will anyone hear in the wide open square the tone of His voice He will not crack apart or rend in pieces a shattered reed or the smoking flax He will not extinguish until He ejects justice from the judicial bench of Divine Law the triumph of the conquest and in the authority and character of His name, foreign races and tribes will have confidence."**

During these days, He went up onto the mountain to pray to Yahuah and He was sitting up the whole night in an oratory prayer of worship to Yahuah. When it became daylight He called to His pupils and summoned and called towards Himself twelve whom He wished and they went off to Him. Yahusha professed them as ambassadors of the Gospel and official commissioners of the Messiah.

He gave to them delegated influence over morally lewd and demonic spirits so too eject them and to relieve all diseases of maladies and moral disabilities and every softness of debility. The names of the twelve delegated ambassadors of the Gospel who were commissioners of the Messiah chosen were: Shim'own (Simon); who was called Kepha (Peter); Andreas (Andrew) his brother; Ya'kov (James) the son of Zabdiy (Zebedee) and Yowchanan (John) his brother, the first cousins of Yahusha; Philippos (Phillip); Bartalmay (Son of Talmay or Bartholomew); Ta'owm (Thomas); Mattithiyah (Matthew) the tax farmer; Ya'kov (James) the son of Cheleph; Thaddaios (Thaddeus); Shim'own the Kna'aniy (Simon the Canaanite); and Yhuwdah Iysh'Qriyowth (Judas Iscariot meaning man from the city of buildings) who also yielded Yahusha the Messiah up.

These twelve Yahusha would send out on a mission having enjoined them with a transmitted message, "Do not go off onto the road of foreign and pagan nations and do not enter into a town of the Shomroniy (Samaritans). But rather travel to the sheep of the family of Yisra'Yah (Israel). Traveling and heralding like a public crier relating these words, 'The royalty, realm and rule of heaven, the eternal abode of Yahuah has approached and has come near!' Relieve the diseases of the feeble. Cleanse scaly lepers. Waken those lying down in death. Eject demonic beings. As a gratuitous sacrificial present you take and hold onto, gratuitously give. Acquire not gold, silver or copper in your belts or pockets. Neither take a wallet or leather pouch for food for the road of two tunic shirts or sandals or a stick for a wand because the toiling teacher is deserving of his nourishment rations and wages. Whatever town with walls or hamlet that you enter into, ascertain who in it is deserving and stay there until you issue forth. When you enter into the residence of a family enfold it in your arms with a salutation. If indeed the residence is deserving let the prosperity of your peace come upon it. But if it is not deserving, let the prosperity of your peace revert back to you."

"Whoever will not receive you or not hear your thoughts on the topic of the Messiah issue out of that residence or that town with walls and shake off violently the blowing dust from your feet. Firmly I relate to you in words as a set discourse, it will be more endurable for the soil of Cdom and Amorah (Sodom and Gomorrah) on the day in front of the judicial bench of Divine Law than that town. Look here! I send you out on a mission like sheep among wolves of white hair. Therefore, be cautious and cunning as snakes and innocent as pigeon doves. Hold in mind and be cautious about the human beings because they will yield you up to the Sanhedrin and they will flog you in their meeting places of the synagogues. You will be led and brought to chief persons of providences and also sovereigns holding the foundation of power on account of Me to be evidence to them and to foreign races. But when they yield you up do not be anxious about in what way or why you will utter in words because it will be given to you in that hour what you are to utter. For this reason, you are not the ones uttering words but the Sacred Breath of your Father who talks through you. Brother will yield up brother to death and father his child. Children will attack their parents and kill them. You will be hated and detested because of My Name. But he who remains until reaching the point of the goal, this one will be delivered and protected."

"When they persecute you in this town with walls, vanish and run away to a different one. I firmly relate to you in words in a set discourse in no way will you conclude your discharge in the town with walls in Yisra'Yah (Israel) until the wish of the Son of Man comes. The pupil is not superior to the instructor or the slave superior to his master. It is satisfactory for the pupil to become in the same manner as his instructor and the slave to be in the same manner as his master. If they call the head of the family Ba'al Zbuwb (meaning lord of the flies), how much of a greater degree those of his relatives? Therefore do not be alarmed or frightened of them because nothing which is covered will have its cover taken off and that which is concealed to privacy will be made known. What words that I relate to you in the dimness of obscurity you shall speak as rays of light. What you hear in your ear herald as a public crier on the roof. You must not be alarmed or frightened of those who slay and kill outright the body but are not able to destroy the vitality of breath. But rather the One who can destroy fully both the vitality of breath and the body in the valley of eternal punishment, hell."

"Are not two little sparrows bartered or sold for a Roman assarion coin? Yet not one of them will fall to the soil of the globe without your Father. Even the hairs of your head are enumerated. Therefore, do not be alarmed or frightened! You surpass many little sparrows. Therefore, anyone who will acknowledge Me in front of human beings then I will acknowledge him in front of My Father who is in heaven, the eternal abode of Yahuah. Whoever will contradict and reject Me in front of human beings then I will also reject him in front of My Father who is in heaven. So do not use the Law to regard that I come to throw peace on the soil of the globe. I did not come to throw peace but a knife of judicial punishment. For this reason, I came to sunder apart and alienate a man from his father and a daughter from her mother and a young veiled married woman from her mother-in-law and a man's hateful adversaries are his own relatives. He who loves father or mother instead of or more than Me is not deserving of Me. Also, He who loves son or daughter instead of or more than Me is not deserving of Me."

"He who does not get a hold of and take his cross of capital punishment to be exposed to death and following My back in the same way as Me is not deserving of Me. He who finds his vitality of breath will have it fully destroyed and he who has the vitality of breath fully destroyed on account of Me will find it. He who receives you receives Me and he who receives Me receives the One who sent me on a mission. He who receives an inspired prophet in the name of the inspired prophet will receive the pay for services of an inspired prophet. He who receives the innocent and holy in the name of the innocent a holy will receive the reward of the innocent and holy. Whoever furnishes a chilly drink from a drinking vessel to one of these small ones in the name of My pupils, I firmly relate to you in words as a set discourse not at all will his pay for services perish." Then Yahusha descended down the mountain with the twelve of them and stood on a level spot and a throng of rabble of His pupils and a large throng of rabble of the people came to hear Him and to be cured from their maladies. Also, those being mobbed and harassed by impure demonic spirits and they were relieved of their diseases. All the throng of rabble sought to touch Him because miraculous power from Him issued forth and cured all.

Yowchanan Matbyl (John the Baptist) heard in bondage from the dungeon of Machaerus about the work and actions of the Anointed Messiah so he summoned calling towards himself two of his disciples. He said to them, ask Yahusha, "Are you the One coming or should we watch in anticipation and wait in hope for someone different?" Then he sent out on a temporary errand his two pupils to Yahusha. When they found Yahusha they said to Yahusha, "*Yowchanan Matbyl* (John the Baptist) sent us out on a mission to You to ask You, are You the One coming or should we watch in anticipation and wait in hope for someone different?" In that very same hour He relieved many from diseases and maladies and disabilities and demonic spirits. To many blind He granted as a favor to see. Yahusha responded and said to them, "Travel back to Yowchanan and announce what you hear and look at; blind ones recover sight and the limping ones tread all around and walk at large. The scaly lepers are cleansed and the deaf of hearing now hear. The corpses of the dead are wakened and aroused from lying in death and the pauper beggars are evangelized with the announcement of the good news of the Gospel. Supremely blest is he whoever does not stumble and be enticed to sin against Me."

As the two men traveled away, Yahusha commenced to teach the throng of rabble with respect to *Yowchanan Matbyl* (John the Baptist), "What did you issue forth for to the wasteland to look closely at, the stem of a reed being rocked and agitated by the wind? But what did you issue forth to see? A man invested and enrobed in a fine soft dress. I don't think so! Those wearing soft fine clothing and indulging in the indulgence of luxury are in the palaces of sovereigns holding the foundations of power. What did you issue out to see, an inspired prophet? Yes, I relate to you in words even one more superabundant than an inspired prophet For this reason, the one around whom it was written and describing in Mal'akiy (Malachi) chapter three verse one, "***I will send out on a mission My messenger in front of Your face who will prepare Your road ahead of time for You.***" Firmly, I tell you not even one has been raised from obscurity among those born of a woman greater than *Yowchanan Matbyl* (John the Baptist)! But the smallest in dignity in the royalty, realm and rule of heaven, the eternal abode of Yahuah are greater than he is. From the days of *Yowchanan Matbyl* (John the Baptist) until just now the royalty, realm and rule of heaven, the eternal abode of Yahuah has been forcibly seizing and the force of energy seize it. All inspired prophets and the Law of Mosheh (Moses) foretold events and spoke under divine inspiration until the time of Yowchanan (John). If you choose to receive it, he is Eliyah (Elijah) He who it was about to come. He having ears to hear, let him hear."

"But what will I compare this generation of age? It is similar to little boys sitting down near the thoroughfares in the market of the public town square and addressing to their comrades saying, 'we played the flute to you and you did not dance in a row or a ring. We bewailed to you but you did not beat your chests in grief and you did not sob with loud wailing! For this reason, *Yowchanan Matbyl* (John the Baptist) neither came eating raised loaves of bread or drinking intoxicating fermented wine and they express in speech, 'He is a demonic being.' The son of Man came eating and drinking and they express in speech, 'Look here, a glutton of a human being and a friend of tax farmers who collect public revenue and of sinners.' Spiritual wisdom of Yahuah was rendered innocent and just by her children, those hearing and the tax farmers who collect the public revenue. They became submerged to make fully wet in baptism the immersion baptism of *Yowchanan Matbyl* (John the Baptist). But the Parash (Pharisee Sect) and the legal experts in Mosaic Law did not perceive the advice of Yahuah, for they themselves had not been submerged to make fully wet in baptism by him."

Shortly after the two pupils reported back to *Yowchanan Matbyl* (John the Baptist) that Yahusha was the Anointed Messiah, Tetrarch Herodes Antipater (Herod Antipas) was induced to hold birthday ceremonies for himself and had the daughter of Herodias dance in motion in the middle of the feasting tables. Through her dancing Herodes Antipater (Herod Antipas) had excited emotions and it was agreeable to him so he acknowledged to her in front of all the guests with an oath to give to her whatever she might ask. She being instigated and forced by her mother said, "Give me in this same spot on a plate the head of *Yowchanan Matbyl* (John the Baptist)!" Now,

Tetrarch Herodes Antipater had Yowchanan seized, retained and bound him and placed him under guard because of Herodias, the ex-wife of the brother of Herodes Antipater, Philippos. *Yowchanan Matbyl* (John the Baptist) publically stated, "It is not right being out in public for you to possess her." Therefore, Tetrarch Herod wishing to kill him outright but he was frightened of the throng of rabble because they held him to be an inspired prophet. Therefore, Herodes was greatly distressed and sad because of the oath and those who reclined in company with him at the meal but he ordered it to be given. So, he sent a dispatch and he decapitated Yowchanan in the guarded place and his head was carried on a plate and was given to the little girl and she carried it to her mother. The pupils of *Yowchanan Matbyl* (John the Baptist) approached the guarded place and lifted up the body and celebrated funeral rites for him. Then they went and announced the news to Yahusha the Messiah. When Yahusha heard that His second cousin had been murdered by Herod, He retired from the mountain and went in a sailing vessel into the location of a wasteland separating Himself on a high hill for privacy to grieve. But when He looked up from deep prayer……………………

13

……..and saw a large crowd coming to Him because they also had heard about it and where He had gone. His pupils approached and came near to Him. He raised up His eyes to His pupils as He opened His mouth and began to teach them a sermon on the mount, "Supremely bless the beggars and paupers because yours is the royalty, realm and rule of Yahuah. Supremely bless those now being famished and carving nourishment because you will be gorged in abundance with food. Supremely bless those sobbing and wailing now because you will laugh with joy. Supremely blest are you when human beings hate and detest you and when they exclude you and demean, rail at, chide and taunt you and eject your name as evil on account of the Son of Man. Be happy and cheerful on that day and skip and jump for joy. For this reason, your pay for services is much in heaven, the eternal abode of Yahuah! For this reason, down in time in the same way their fathers did these things to the inspired prophets."

"But woe for you abounding with wealth because you have received in full your solace! Woe for those when all people speak by word or writing well of you. For this reason down in time their fathers in the same way did to the religious imposters and counterfeit prophets. I relate to you in words as a set discourse to those hearing, love your hateful adversaries even though they are actively hostile. Do well to those full of hatred and detest and persecute you. Speak well of and bless with a benediction those cursing doom on you and pray to Yahuah for those insulting and threatening your character with slander. To those thumping you on the jawbone or cheek of your face with repeated blows, present also your other side. From those who lift and take away your outer dress, do not prevent or stop them from possessing also your tunic shirt. To everyone asking you to give and from those taking your things do not demand them back. As you prefer that human beings do to you also you do to them similarly. If you love those loving you what graciousness of gratitude is there to you? For these reasons even the sinners love those that love them. If you be a well-doer as a favor or duty to those being well doers to you, what graciousness of gratitude is there to you? For this reason even the sinners do the same. If you loan on interest to whom you expect to receive back in full, what graciousness of gratitude is that to you? For this reason, even the sinners loan on interest to sinners, in order that they receive back in full similarly."

After the Sermon on the Mount summer came and Yahusha entered into the town of Kaphernahuwm (Capernaum). There a slave of a captain of one hundred men who possessed physical badness and was about to finish life and was valued very much by his master. Hearing with respect to Yahusha the Centurion sent out to Him with senior members of the Sanhedrin of the Yhudiy (Jews) and requested Him that He would cure his slave saying, "Master, my boy slave child, a paralytic, has been thrown down violently in my residence and is being terribly tortured." The senior members of the Yhudiy (Jews) implored Him earnestly, begging, "He is deserving whom presented this thing because he loves our race and he constructed our synagogue for the assemblage of persons." Therefore, Yahusha said, "I will come and relieve him of his disease." Yet even now He was not at a far distance from the residence and the captain of one hundred Roman soldiers who was with some Yhudiy (Jewish) friend stated, "Master do not be harassed. I am not fit in character that You should enter under the roof of my thatched deck. Consequently, I did not deem towards myself to be fit for You to come. Instead, just speak Your thoughts as the Messiah and my boy child servant will be cured. I understand because even I am a human being assigned under the privilege of delegated influence, possessing under myself warriors that camp out and I express in speech to this person 'Travel' and he travels. To a different one I might say, 'Come' and he comes. Even to my slave I might say 'Do this thing' and he does it."

Yahusha heard these things and admired him. He twisted around and said to the throng of rabble united on the road with Him, "I relate to you in words, not even in all of Yisra'Yah (Israel) have I found such a vast amount of moral conviction of religious truth of Yahuah to rely upon the Messiah for salvation. Many will arrive from the rising of the sun in the east and the setting of the sun in the west and will recline with Abraham, Yitschaq (Isaac) and Yisra'Yah (Israel/Jacob) in the royalty, realm and rule of heaven, the eternal abode of Yahuah. But the sons of the royalty, realm and rule will be ejected into the exterior obscure shadiness. There will be lamentation and grating of the teeth." Yahusha then turned to the captain of one hundred men and said with comforting words, "Retire as if sinking out of sight and as you had faith and trusted your spiritual well-being to the Messiah let it come into being to you as you have requested." Then those that were dispatched with the Centurion returned to the dwelling and found the slave in sound health and had been cured that very hour.

Exactly on the successive day, Yahusha traveled into a town called Na'ah (Nain) meaning 'pasture home' and journeyed together with Him were His pupils and a great throng of rabble. When He approached near to the gate of the town, being carried forth for burial one having died, an only son born to his mother who was a widow. An ample amount of a throng of rabble of the town was united with her for companionship. Seeing her, the Messiah felt sympathy and His bowels yearned with pity for her. He said to her, "Do not sob with wailing." He approached near and touched the funeral coffin and those sustaining the coffin stood still. Yahusha said, "Youth, to you I lay forth words. Rouse up from lying in death!" At once the dead corpse sat up and commenced to talk. Then Yahusha gave him to his mother. All watching were taken aback and put in fear and they were all glorifying Yahuah relating in words, "A great inspired prophet has been awakened among us and Yahuah has come to see and relieve His people." Word of this thing issued forth in all of Yhuwdah (Judea) with respect to Him and in all the surrounding regions.

On a hot summer's day when He was teaching, Yahusha began to rail on the town with walls in which the largest number of his miraculous powers had come into being because they had not reconsidered to think differently and repent saying, "Woe to you Chorazin! Woe to you Beyth Tsayad (Bethsaida)! Because if in Tsor (Tyre) and Tsiydown (Sidon) the miracles that came into being in you, they would have reconsidered to think differently some time ago in mohair sackcloth and ashes, Nevertheless, I relate in words to you, it will be more endurable for Tsor (Tyre) and Tsiydown (Sidon) on the day standing in front of the bench of divine judicial law than for you! Even you Kaphernachuwm (Capernaum), who will be elevated to heaven, the eternal abode of Yahuah? Your cause will go down to hell. Because if in Cdom (Sodom) the power of miracles that came into being in you would have happened there, it would have stayed until today. However, I state plainly the soil of Cdom (Sodom) will be more endurable on the day standing in front of the bench of divine judicial law than for you."

Then Yahusha raised His hands towards the crowd and heaven saying, "I acknowledge and agree fully with You, Father, Master of heaven and of the globe because You concealed away fully to keep secret these things from the wise and those with keen perception and instead took off the cover and disclosed them to simple minded persons Yes, Father in this way it came into being in front of You. All things were yielded up and entrusted to Me by My Father. No one becomes fully acquainted with the Son except the Father and no one becomes fully acquainted with the Father except the Son and to whomever the Son is willing to take the cover off and disclose Him. Come to Me all who are feeling fatigued from working hard and overburdened with spiritual anxiety of ceremony and I will give you rest and refresh you. Take my yoke of servitude upon you and discern from Me because I am gentle and humiliated in the thoughts of my heart. You will find intermission and recreation of the vitality of your breath because My yoke of servitude is useful and the task of My freight is light and easy."

A week later a certain member of the Parash (Pharisee Sect) requested Him that He eat with him. After entering into the residence of the Parash (Pharisee), He leaned back on the sitting cushion. Then when a woman who was in the town, a sinner, recognized that He had reclined for the meal in the residence of the Parash, she provided an alabaster perfume vase of myrrh perfumed oil and stood behind His feet sobbing and commenced to drown His feet with her tears and with the hair of her head she wiped dry and kissed earnestly His feet and oiled them with the myrrh perfumed oil. The Parash (Pharisee) who called Him, saw this and he thought within himself, "If He were an inspired prophet He would know who and what the woman who touches Him is because she is a sinner." Yahusha responded to his thoughts and said to him, "Shim'own (Simon) I have something to say to you." Shim'own the Parash (Pharisee) said, "Instructor speak." So Yahusha said, "There were two indebted persons to a certain lender. The one owed five hundred denarii (eighty dollars) and the different one fifty denarii (eight dollars). They did not possess anything to pay back so both he granted as a favor in kindness and pardoned them. Accordingly, which one of them would love him more?" Shim'own (Simon) responded, "I assume to whom he pardoned in kindness the more." Yahusha answered "You decided correctly!" Then twisting around to the woman He made known His thoughts to Shim'own, "Look at the woman! I entered into your residence. You did not give water on My feet but she moistened with a shower of her tears on My feet and wiped them dry with her hair. You did not give Me a kiss but from when I entered she has not stopped earnestly kissing My feet. You did not oil My head with olive oil but she oiled My feet with myrrh perfumed oil. For this reason I relate to you in words of a set discourse, the many sins of her are sent away because she loved much, but to who loves little, little is sent away." Then Yahusha said to her, "Your sins are sent away." Those reclining in company with Him at the meal commenced to lay forth words inside themselves, "Who is this? Who even sends away sins?' Yahusha once again addressed the woman saying, "Your moral conviction of religious truth of Yahuah and reliance upon the Messiah for salvation has saved and delivered you. Travel in peace."

The rest of the autumn before the Feast of Tabernacles Yahusha was traveling through every town and hamlet, heralding as a public crier the divine truth of the Gospel and announcing the good news to evangelize the Gospel of the royalty, realm and rule of Yahuah and the twelve were with Him. Also, certain women who were relieved of their diseases from demonic spirits and feeble maladies, Miryam (Mary) called Magealene from whom seven demonic beings issued out and Yowanna (Joanna) wife of Chouzas, the domestic manager of Tetrarch Herodes Antipater and Showshannnah (Susanna) and many more different ones who were attendants to Him out of their property and possessions. Then they went back to Kaphernachuwm (Capernaum) by the sea.

While there in that town, there was tendered to Him a human being exercised by a demon also being blind and dumb of speech. He relieved him of his diseases, thus the one that was blind and dumb of speech could both talk and look at things. All the throng of rabble became astounded and related in words, "Is this not the Son of David?" The Parash (Pharisee Sect) who had come up from the Great City of Yruwshalaim (Jerusalem) having heard this became indignant and said, "This one ejects demonic beings by the power of Ba'al Zhuwb, the dung fly god of Satan, who is first in the power of rank of the demonic beings!" But knowing their deliberations Yahusha spoke to them, "Every dominion disunited against its self is laid to waste and every town with walls or family disunited against itself will not stand. If Satan the arch enemy of good ejects Satan then he is disunited against himself. Accordingly, in what way will his realm stand? If I eject the demonic beings by Ba'al Zhuwb the god of dung flies, then by whom do your sons eject demons? Therefore, they will be your judges. But if I by the Sacred Breath (Holy Spirit) the finger of Yahuah eject demonic beings, then it is concluded that the anticipated royalty, realm and rule of Yahuah has arrived upon you!"

"In what way can any person enter into the residence of the strong forcible one and plunder his equipment and wife as she contributes to the usefulness of her husband. Unless first he binds the forcible one and then he will plunder the residence and family. I also, tell you that if the strong are equipped fully with the armor of guards his yard of the mansion open to the wind, his possessions and wealth are in peace. But when the one stronger than him attacks, the stronger one will subdue him and take off his full armor on which he relied upon and will distribute it throughout the crowd his stripped booty. Therefore, He who does not accompany and become joined to Me is against Me and He who does not lead together and collect with Me, dissipates and puts to flight becoming a liberal waste. Because this one thing I will relate to you in a set discourse. Every sin and vilification against Yahuah will be sent forth from the human beings. However, vilification against the Sacred Breath of Yahuah will not be sent forth and forgiven. Whoever speaks their thoughts and motives against the Son of Man, it will be sent forth from him. However, whoever speaks by word or writing against the Sacred Breath will not be sent forth not even in this age or not even in the expected one."

"Either make the tree good and its plucked fruit good or make the tree rotten or worthless and its plucked fruit rotten and worthless because by the plucked fruit the tree is known. Offspring of poisonous snakes! How are you able to talk about good things since yourselves being hurtful, evil, malicious, vicious, and of the devil? For this reason out of the surplus and superabundance of the heart the mouth utters words. The good human being ejects forth the good things out of the good deposit of wealth of the thoughts and feelings of the heart and the evil, guilty, derelict and sinning human being ejects forth evil, derelict and vicious things out of the hurtful, evil and devilish deposit of wealth. I relate to you in words that every lazy and useless word that human beings may utter, they will give up their thoughts and motives with respect to it on the day of justice in front of the judicial bench of Divine Law. For by your thoughts and motives you will be rendered just and innocent and by your thoughts and motives you will be judged against and pronounced guilty!"

After Yahusha put the scribes and Parash (Pharisee Sect) in their place, He was invited inside a house to eat bread and to continue preaching. However, the scribes and Parash followed inside and they still continued to test the Messiah by saying, "Instructor, we wish from you a supernatural medication miracle to see." Yahusha not giving into becoming a mere sideshow responded firmly, "An evil and adulterous generation of age searches, craves and demands and indication of the supernatural. A supernatural indication miracle will not be given to it except the supernatural indication of Yonah (Jonah) the inspired prophet. Exactly like Yonah (Jonah) was in the abdomen cavity of the huge fish for three days and three nights in this way the Son of Man will be in the heart of the soil for three days and three nights. The men of Niynveh will stand up in front of the bench of the judicial Divine Law with this generation of age on the Day of Damnation Judgment and will judge a sentence against it because they thought differently afterwards and reconsidered their moral compunction at the proclamation of the gospel by Yonah. See here! One more in quality than Yonah (Jonah) is here in this spot! The Queen of the Southwest will be roused from death before the judicial bench of Divine Law with this generation of age on the Day of Damnation Judgment and will judge a sentence against it because she came from the extremity of the soil of the globe to hear the spiritual wisdom of Shlomoh (Solomon). Look here! One more in quality than Shlomoh (Solomon) is here in this spot!" This made the religious scribes and Parash (Pharisee Sect) grumble among themselves because the truth that was spoken by the Messiah made them feel ashamed and their conscience plead guilty.

As they grumbled amongst themselves Yahusha continued teaching, "But when a demonic spirit issues forth and away from a human being he travels through waterless and dry spots of space seeking intermission and recreation yet does not find it. Then he thinks to himself I will revert back to harangue my dwelling place from where I issued forth. Then coming he finds it vacant and on leisure taking a holiday swept with a broom and decorated of the world. Then he travels and associates himself with seven other demonic spirits more evil than him and entering resides to house permanently there. The final stages of the human being become more evil and aggravated than at the first. Thus it will also be with this evil and vicious generation of age!" It came to be as He had finished saying these things, a certain woman raised up her voice out of the throng of rabble and said to Him, "Supremely blest is the cavity of the matrix that gave birth to You and the breasts which you suckled." But He said, "*Lo*! (No) supremely blest are those hearing the Messiah of Yahuah and guarding to obey it!"

Then He concluded His instruction by teaching, "Not even one having set on fire a portable lamp places it to be private and concealed or under the dry measure that holds one-fourth of a bushel (15 pounds) but on the lamp stand in order that those entering may see the brilliancy of the light. The lamp of the body is the eye. Then when your eye is clear also all of your body is lustrous and well lit. But when it is evil also your body is full of darkness. Accordingly, take aim at and regard, lest the shining rays of light in you becomes obscure shadiness. If your whole body is lustrous and well-lit not possessing any part with darkness all will be lustrous and well lit, as when the lamp like the glare of lightning will shed rays of bright shining light in you."

A short time later when the Messiah had finished teaching but was still talking to the throng of rabble inside the house, His mother Miryam (Mary) and His brothers stood outdoors, seeking to talk to Him. His family had heard about Him being here and issued out to use strength to seize Him stating, "He is out of wits and insane! He possesses a demonic spirit!" They were not able to meet with Him through the crowd, so they stood outside the door calling for Him by name. Then someone said to Yahusha, "Your mother and Your brothers are standing outdoors wishing to see and speak to You." Yahusha responded and said to the one talking to Him, "Who is My mother and who are My brothers?" Then He extended His hand towards His pupils and He announced, "Look here! My mother and my brothers! For this reason, whoever does the purpose and decrees of My Father who is in heaven, the eternal abode of Yahuah he is My brother and sister and mother"

The next morning as the sun was just beginning to peek its head above the pinks, oranges and violets in the eastern horizon, Yahusha issued out of the residence and He sat down by the sea to pray. Then a large throng of rabble collected towards Him, thus He walked on into the sailing vessel and sat down while the throng of rabble stood on the beach of the sea with the waves dashing. Then He uttered seven things in parables of common life conveying a moral truth saying, "One scattering to sow began to sow. In his scattering to sow some seeds in fact fell beside the road and flying birds came and devoured them. Yet different ones fell upon the rock like places in whichever spots and they did not have much soil. At once they germinated and started up out of the ground because of not possessing deep soil. When the sun rouse up and the young sprouts were burnt because of not possessing any roots, so they shriveled up. Other seeds fell upon the thorns and the thrones grew up and overgrew them and choked them out. Finally, some fell upon the good soil and gave plucked fruit, one a hundred and one sixty and one thirty. Those possessing ears to hear let him hear!"

The pupils came to Him and asked, "Why do You talk in common life parables of truth to them?" Yahusha answered, "Because to you it has been given to know the secret mysteries of the royalty, realm and rule of heaven, the eternal abode of Yahuah, but to those it has not been given. For whoever possesses it will be given to him and he will have a super-abounding excess but whoever possess not, even what he possesses will be lifted up and taken away from him! Because of this thing, I utter in words to them in parables of common life of moral truth because seeing they do not see and hearing they do not hear or comprehend. The prediction of Ysha'Yah (Isaiah) is accomplished upon them from chapter six verses nine and ten, **'In hearing you will hear but in no way comprehend and seeing you will see but by no way know. For the heart of this people has become calloused with thick fat and with heavy ears they heard and their eyes were shut, lest they see with their eyes and hear with their ears and with their hearts comprehend and I will cure them."** But supremely blest are your eyes because they see and your ears because they hear. For this reason I firmly state that many inspired prophets and holy ones set their hearts upon and longed for to see what you see and to hear what you here, but they did not hear."

Then the pupils with the twelve asked Yahusha what was the meaning of the parable of the sowing seed. Yahusha said, "If you do not understand this simple parable then how are you going to understand the rest of the parables? Hear, you therefore the parable of common life conveying a moral truth of the one who scattered the seed. Everyone that hears the subject of the royalty, realm and rule of the Messiah and does not comprehend it, then the devil comes and seizes and takes away the message of divine expression of the Messiah that which was scattered to be sown in his heart. This is the scattered seed by the road. The scattered seed on the rocky places, this is the one who hears the message of divine expression of the Messiah and at once takes it and gets a hold of it with cheerfulness and delight. This person does not possess any root in himself but is for the occasion only and temporary. When pressure or persecution comes about through the topic of the Messiah, he is at once tripped up into apostasy and enticed to sin. He who is scattered in the thorns, this is the one hearing the message of the Messiah and the distraction of evil anxiety fear of this age and the delusions of the fullness of the wealth of money and valuable possessions and circumstances about the remaining longing for what is forbidden enters in and completely strangles the message of the Messiah, and it becomes barren. But the one in which the seed was sown on good soil this is the one hearing the message of the Messiah and comprehends it, who then becomes fertile and makes in fact a hundred, one sixty and one thirty."

Then Yahusha the Messiah presented the second parable, "The royalty, realm and rule of the heaven, the eternal abode of Yahuah is compared to a human being scattering good seed in his fields. But as the human being laid down to rest and fell asleep, his hatful adversary came and scattered darnel, being false grain in the middle of the wheat and then departed. When the vegetation of the garden germinated and sprouted to yield its fruit and then made its fruit, then the darnel being false grain also showed up. The slaves of the head of the family approached and came near and said to him, 'Master, did you not scatter good seed in your field of the farm in the country? From where and why then does it possess darnel the false grain?' The head of the family made known his thoughts, 'An odious and hateful adversary, a human being, did this!' Then the slaves said to him, 'Will you have us go off and collect the false grain?' The head of the family firmly said, 'No, lest while collecting the darnel the false grain you might uproot the wheat with them. Let both grow up together to the point of reaping the crop. Then in the proper time of reaping of the crop I will say to the harvesters, collect first the darnel, the false grain and bind them into bundles in order to burn them, but the wheat collect together into My granary"

Yahusha continued and taught parable number three, "The royalty, realm and rule of heaven, the eternal abode of Yahuah is compared to a kernel of mustard which a human being took and scattered in his field on the country farm. The mustard seed, which in fact is the smallest in size than all the seeds of the earth but when it is grown is larger than must dug vegetables. It becomes a tree. Therefore, the birds of the sky come and remain in its boughs." He took a quick breath and began parable number four, "The royalty, realm and rule of heaven, the eternal abode of Yahuah is similar to the fermentation of yeast boiling up. A woman took and incorporated it in with three dry measure of ground flour until the whole thing was fermented." He continued to teach in parables of common life conveying a moral truth to verify the prediction of what was spoken through the inspired prophet in Thillah (Psalm) chapter seventy-eight verse two, *"I will open My mouth in parables of common life conveying a moral truth. I will belch and speak forth concealed and covered things since the conception of the world."*

Yahusha was weary so he sent away the throng of rabble, got out of the sailing vessel and went back to the residence of a family. As He sat down on the reclining cushion, His pupils came to Him requesting, "Define and expound upon to us the parable of the darnel, the false grain of the field of the country farm." He answered them, "The one scattering the good seed is the Son of Man. The field on the country farm is the world including its inhabitants. These good seeds are the sons of the royalty, realm and rule but the darnel the false grain are the sons of the devil, Satan. The odious and hateful adversary who scattered them is Satan. The reaping of the crop is the completion of the age and the harvesters are messengers who bring tidings known as angels. The darnel being false grain is collected and is burned and consumed fully by fire like lightning. In this way it will be at the entire completion of this age. The Son of Man will send out His messenger angels and they will collect out of His royalty, realm and rule all the displeasures of sin being trap sticks for snares and those who do wickedness and violate the Law. They will violently throw them into the furnace of lightening fire. There will be lamentation and grating of teeth. Then the equitable in character or actions being innocent and holy will be brilliantly bright and will shine in the same manner as the sunlight in the royalty, realm and rule of their Father. He having ears to hear let him hear!"

After the evening meal, a large crowd had gathered once more outside the residence so Yahusha went to the door and stood under the thatched roof and began speaking to those gathered. He then taught parable number five, "Once more the royalty, realm and rule of heaven, the eternal abode of Yahuah is similar to a concealed deposit of wealth in the field of a country farm which a human being found and covered it. Then from the cheerfulness and delight of it he withdraws as if sinking out of sight and he barters as a peddler to sell all the things, whatever he possesses. Next, he goes to the market and redeems it by purchasing that field on the country farm." He immediately continued with parable number six, "Once more the royalty realm and rule of heaven the eternal abode of Yahuah is similar to a human being, a wholesale tradesman seeking beautiful and valuable pearls from the oyster, who found one extremely valuable pearl. He departed and disposed of all his things as merchandise, everything he possessed and went to the market and redeemed it by purchasing it." As the throng of rabble was very silent and hanging onto every word that proceeded from His mouth, He concluded with parable number seven, "Once more the royalty, realm and rule of heaven, the eternal abode of Yahuah, is similar to a fishing seine thrown into the sea and every 'kin' was collected together which when the net was crammed full and hauled onto the beach of the sea where the waves dash and sitting down the good fish were collected into receptacle pails but the worthless and rotten fish were violently thrown out. In this way it will be at the entire completion of the age. The messenger angels will issue forth and will set off a boundary in the middle of the equitable in character and actions being innocent and holy, from the evil ones of the devil who will be violently thrown into the furnace of the fire like lightening. There will be lamentation and grating of the teeth."

Since it was getting late, Yahusha dismissed the crowd and went back inside the residence with His pupils. As soon as the door was shut He turned around facing His pupils and asked, "Did you comprehend all these things?" They said to Him, "*Ken* (Yes)." Then Yahusha said to them, "Because of this thing, every scribe becoming a disciple into the royalty, realm and rule of heaven the eternal abode of Yahuah is similar to a human being, the head of a family who ejects forth out of his deposit of wealth new and fresh and antique and worn out."

That evening Yahusha informed the twelve and His pupils that the Sacred Breath (Holy Spirit) was nudging Him to move on from there and go across the sea. The next morning, since the host family knew that the Messiah was leaving prepared a massive breakfast before hitting the road. They had piping hot *latkes* (fried potato pancakes with sour cream and apple sauce) and mouth-watering *rugelach* (flaky pastries spread with cinnamon sugar and chocolate chips, rolled and baked). The big fisherman Kepha (Peter) could not stop stuffing himself full of the *blintz* (thin fried egg pancakes wrapped around a sweet mixture of farmer's cheese, potato and fruit filling rolled in cinnamon sugar). The favorite of the Messiah was the *hamantashen* (triangular pastries filled with poppy seed, onions, prune paste and fruit jams). Of course there were baskets of bright orange fresh picked oranges, large yellow grapefruit, and clumps of deep purple grapes. After what seemed to be an endless banquet of sweet pastries, fruit and egg pancakes, Yahusha took time to thank their hosts and when all the farewells had been said Yahusha raised His arms towards the hosts and pronounced the *HaShama* (the hearing), "*Shama Yisra'Yah Yahuah Yah Yahuah Echad* (Hear, Israel, Yahuah our God is one Yahuah). He followed it up with *HaGadowl Mitsvah* (the greatest command), "*Ahab Yahuah Yah, kol lebab, kol nephesh, kol m'od* (Love Yahuah your God with all your heart and with all our vitality of breath and with your whole strength)." The five year old son of the host quickly said, "I know those because they were my Torah lesson from the sacred book of *Dabar* (Deuteronomy, meaning 'spoken words') chapter six verses four and five!" Yahusha patted the little black curly haired boy on the head and everyone waved good-by as they headed down the dusty road towards the sea So it came to be when Yahusha had completed and concluded all these parables of common life, He removed Himself from there the next day following the parables and left that town.

14

As Yahusha and His pupils, along with the twelve were headed towards the seashore, one scribe approached and said to Him, "Instructor, I will accompany You as a disciple and travel on the same road as You wherever You go." Yahusha stopped and said to him, "The cunning foxes have burrows for lurking places and the flying birds of the sky have perches to camp in but the Son of Man has not anywhere to recline His head." Then someone else who was following yelled, "Mister, first allow me to go off and celebrate the funeral rites of my father." Yahusha looked up and said, "Accompany Me as a disciple and send the dead corpses to celebrate the funeral rites of the dead, themselves." Finally, He walked into the sailing vessel with the twelve and some of the pupils as many as would fit. Other followers got into different smaller sailing vessels.

    The sailing vessel was plunging through the water and they had gone a great distance out to sea, when a great commotion of a squall of a whirlwind gale blowing in the air and earthquake of the ground came into being on the sea so as to cover up the sailing vessel by the swelling curved waves that were bursting and toppling over the sides of the vessel. The swelling and curved waves continued to billow and burst, toppling with great force being thrown into the sailing vessel beginning to fill it up entirely with water. However, Yahusha was on the stern (back) of the sailing vessel and had laid down to rest and had fallen asleep into a deep slumber with His head on a cushion. His disciples approached near to Him and they woke Him up from

His sleep screaming through the wind and rain, "Master, save us and protect us! We are perishing! Is it of no interest or concern to You that we are perishing?" He looked at their fearful faces now being wakened fully and sternly replied, "Why are you timid and faithless? You are incredulous and lack confidence in the Messiah." Then at that time, He rose up from His sleep and He admonished and forbade the wind and He said to the sea, "Hush! Be muzzled!" Then the wind relaxed and there was a great tranquility. The human beings were in admiration and awe with a great alarm and fright were saying to one another, "What is this that even the winds and the sea listen to Him as a subordinate and conform to the authority of His commands?"

When they came across the sea to their intended destination into the territory of the Girgashiy known as Gadara, two human beings exercised by demons issued out from the remembrance graves and encountered Him on the shore. They were dangerous and furious, so as no one was able to come near or approach that road. The strongest one did not wear any clothing and made his permanent residence in the remembrance graves and no one was able to bind him not even with a manacle of iron to fasten his hands together or a fetter of iron to fasten his feet together. Many times he had been bound with shackles for his feet and manacles of iron to fasten his hands together and the manacles of iron had been severed by him and the fetters of iron had been crushed and shattered completely. No one was able to tame him. Throughout all the night and the day he was croaking like a screaming raven with loud shrieks among the mountains and in the burial places. He also chopped down on his body and mangled himself with stones. They shrieked like a croaking raven screaming and hissing in a hollow tone of voice. When the stronger one saw Yahusha from a distance, he hastily ran and bowed the knee to prostrate himself in homage to do reverence and adoration.

Then he croaked like a screaming raven shrieking with a great bestial tone saying, "What are You to us Yahusha, Son of Yahuah? What do You want with me, Yahusha Son of Yahuah in the highest of the heavens? I solemnly enjoin You by Yahuah not to torture me. Have you come here in this spot before the proper time to torture us?" Then Yahusha commanded, "Issue forth, demonic spirit out of the human being! What is your name?" The demon responded, "Legion is my name because we are many. Do not send us out into an empty expanse or the bottomless pit of the dry regions of the dead in hell." At a distance from them on the mountain was a large drove of grazing hogs in the pasture. All the evil demons of supernatural spirits implored Him saying, "If you reject us, allow us to go off into that drove of hogs!" Yahusha commanded, "Withdraw and lead yourselves under!" Then the demonic spirits issued forth from the human beings and went off into the drove of hogs. Instantly, all of the drove of hogs dashed and plunged down the overhanging precipice cliff into the sea and died off in the water. There were about two thousand grazing hogs and they wheezed as they were drowning in the sea.

Those who were pasturing ran away and vanished. They went off into the town with walls and announced to them and the country farms all these things and the things about those exercised with demons. Then the entire town issued forth with clubs to have a meeting with Yahusha. The town folk became spectators of the strong one that had been exercised by the demon now sitting down at the feet of Yahusha, dressed and sound of sane mind. This is the one that had been possessed by the legion and they were frightened and in awe. When they saw him they implored Yahusha to change His place away from their boundary lines of their frontier. So, Yahusha entered into the sailing vessel and the strong one that had been exercised by demons, invoked Him that he would be with Him as a companion. But Yahusha did not allow him to go forth with Him instead instructing, "Withdraw to your dwelling to those of you and announce in detail to them what the Master has done to you, and had compassion of divine grace on you" Then the man departed and commenced to herald as a public crier the divine truth of the Gospel in Dekapolis, the ten city region how much Yahusha did to him and all were in admiration.

Yahshua and all the sailing vessels returned to the western shore and there to greet then was the throng of rabble to welcome Him back because they were waiting, watching with anticipation in hope for Him. As He was being welcomed back to the shore one with political rank and power as a director of the synagogue service by the name of Ya'iyr (Jairus) came and prostrated himself in homage for reverence and adoration to Him said, "My daughter and my only child just now is about to finish life, but come and put Your hand on her and she will live." Yahusha rose up out of the sailing vessel and accompanying Him were the twelve and also His pupils. The crowd was so large it was pressing Him on all sides. Now then a woman hemorrhaging with a flowing flux of blood for twelve years and had experienced many sensations of pain by many physicians and had consuming expenses that devoured all her things. Yet, nothing from the physicians benefited her but rather made the flow become more aggravated and evil. She had heard about Yahusha and approached from the rear and touched the tassel of His prayer shawl. She had thought to herself, *'If only I could touch His prayer shawl I will be delivered"* At once her gushing fountain of blood dried up and she knew that within her body that she was cured of the disease.

Instantly, Yahusha became fully acquainted with Himself that the force of power had issued forth from out of Him. Yahusha having reversed around to the throng of rabble said, "Who touched My prayer shawl?" However, all denied it. Then Kepha (Peter) said to Him, "Look at the throng of rabble crowding and compressing You on all sides, and You ask who touched Me?" Yahusha responded, "Someone touched Me because I knew miraculous power issued forth from Me." He looked all around to see the one having done this. The woman being frightened and trembling with fear, knowing what had come into being in her, came and fell towards Him, gently prostrating herself in homage and spoke to Him all the truth. He saw her and said, "Be of good cheer daughter! Your moral conviction for religious truth and your reliance upon the Messiah for salvation has delivered you." That woman was delivered and protected from that hour.

As He was speaking to the woman, some came from the residence of the director of synagogue services saying to Ya'iyr (Jairus), "Your daughter has died off. Why still harass the Instructor?" At once, Yahusha heard what was said and uttered words, saying to the director of synagogue services, "Do not be frightened, merely have faith and entrust your spiritual well-being to the Messiah." Then Yahusha came into the residence of Ya'iyr (Jairus) and did not allow anyone to accompany Him inside except Kepha (Peter), Ya'kov (James) and Yowchanan (John) the brother of Ya'kov (James). They saw a disturbance of sobbing and wailing loudly and much shouting to call attention. Also, they witnessed the flute players and the crowd causing a tumultuous disturbance. He raised His voice saying, "Why do you make such a tumult and clamor in a disturbance and sob loudly. Get out of here because the little girl has not died off but she has laid down to rest and fallen asleep." Then the throng of rabble causing the disturbance laughed Him down and derided Him. However, once the crowd had been ejected outside the residence

Yahusha received near the father and mother of the child and those with Him and entered the spot where the child was reclining as a corpse. He used strength and seized her hand and said, "*Taleh quwm* (Lamb rise)!" At once, the little girl stood up and walked at large. She was twelve years old. After He roused the little girl from the sleep of death, they were at once astounded and filled with great ecstasy of bewilderment. Yahusha largely ordered them that no one should know this thing that happened and instructed them to give her something to eat. Following this event, the rumor of His fame issued forth into the entire region.

Yahusha went away from there late that afternoon and two blind ones were on the road calling out, "Have compassion of divine grace on us, Son of David." When He got to the next town, He went into a residence and the blind ones had followed and approached and came near to Him. Yahusha inquired of them, "Do you have faith and entrust your spiritual well-being in the Messiah that I am able to do this?" They broke the silence and said to Him, "Yes Supreme in Authority." Then He touched their eyes and said, "According to your conviction of religious truth and reliance upon the Messiah for salvation let it come into being to you." Then their eyes were opened up. Yahusha sternly warned them, "Discern clearly that no one knows about this." Instead, they issued forth reporting thoroughly and divulged Him in all the territory. As Yahusha was issuing forth others rendered to Him a man dumb of speech and exercised by demons. Having ejected the demonic beings the man dumb of speech began to utter words. The throng of rabble admired Him saying, "This has never been seen in this way in all of Yisra'Yah (Israel)." However, the Parash (Pharisee Sect) said mean words, "We have said it before. Only by the first in rank and power of the demonic beings this imposter ejects the demonic beings."

Just as the year was ending in 28 AD on the Roman calendar during the early winter, Yahusha came to His native town, His father-land of Nazareth. He taught them in their synagogue, the meeting place of the assemblage of persons, so that they were struck with astonishment even stating, "From what source did this person obtain spiritual wisdom and the miraculous power to do miracles? Is this not the son of the craftsman in wood? Is not his mother called Miryam (Mary) and His brothers, Ya'kov (James), Yowceph (Joseph), Shim'own (Simon) and Yhuwdah (Judas or Jude)? His sisters are they all not with us? Accordingly, from what source did He happen to possess all these things?" They were displeased and stumbled into the apostasy of the enticement to sin towards Him. However, Yahusha said to them, "Is not an inspired prophet dishonored or without honor only in his native town of his fatherland, and in his family?" Thus He did not do there many miracles except on a puny number of those lacking health and He relieved them of their diseases by laying His hands on them. He wondered about their faithlessness and disbelief and unfaithfulness of disobedience.

As the year of 28 AD ended on the Roman calendar, the dark lord Satan ranted and raved while licking his wounds from the last encounter he had with Yahusha. He shrieked in a low hissing bestial tone, "Who does this miracle worker Yahusha think He is anyway. Just because His name means Yahuah's Salvation does He truly believe that He is the Son of Yahuah, the restored fellowship of mankind to Yahuah? How could Yahuah stoop so low to become a pitiful human being? This Yahusha must be stopped at all costs. Do you hear me you cowardly minions of the dark!" Then the dark lord seized two unsuspecting spirits by the throats and threw them into his evil black cauldron whose fire had been kindled again. As their gurgling subsided and bubbles raised to the top of the thick brew of black sewage in the cauldron, Satan screeched at the top of his voice, "The new year of 29 AD belongs to me and none other. Do you hear me! No more cowering to His name! You will not be ejected by Him from human beings again! Anyone scampering back to me in defeat will be sentenced to the driest regions of this pit of hell. Do I make myself clear? Doubt and Deception must rule on earth!" Then he stomped his foot sending shock waves throughout the ranks of the demonic underworld. The putrid death smell of his ranting breath overflowed from his kingdom of darkness towards the hard hearts and lustful eyes of earth.

"Unseen Footsteps of Jesus"
OLAM HABA
(Future World)
Mysteries Book 1- "Pre-Dawn"
Jerry Ayers

"Unseen Footsteps of Jesus"
OLAM HABA
(Future World)
Mysteries Book 2- "The Dawning"
Jerry Ayers

"Unseen Footsteps of Jesus"
OLAM HABA
(Future World)
Mysteries Book 3- "The Sunrise"
Jerry Ayers

"Unseen Footsteps of Jesus"
OLAM HABA
(Future World)
Mysteries Book 4- "The Rising Sun"
Jerry Ayers

"Unseen Footsteps of Jesus"
OLAM HABA
(Future World)
Mysteries Book 5- "Storm Clouds"
Jerry Ayers

"Unseen Footsteps of Jesus"
OLAM HABA
(Future World)
Mysteries Book 6- "A Silver Lining"
Jerry Ayers

"Unseen Footsteps of Jesus"
OLAM HABA
(Future World)
Mysteries Book 7- "The Sunset"
Jerry Ayers

OLAM HABA
(Future World)
Jerry Ayers